GENESIS to REVELATION
JOSHUA
JUDGES
RUTH
RAY NEWELL

A Comprehensive Verse-by-Verse Exploration of the Bible

GENESIS to REVELATION

JOSHUA
JUDGES
RUTH

RAY NEWELL

GENESIS TO REVELATION SERIES:
JOSHUA, JUDGES, RUTH
PARTICIPANT

Copyright© 1982 by Graded Press
Revised Edition Copyright © 1997 by Abingdon Press
Updated and Revised Edition Copyright © 2018 by Abingdon Press
All rights reserved.

No part of this work may be reproduced or transmitted in any form or by any means, electronic or mechanical, including photocopying and recording, or by any information or retrieval system, except as may be expressly permitted in the 1976 Copyright Act or in writing from the publisher. Requests for permission should be addressed in writing to Permissions, The United Methodist Publishing House, 2222 Rosa L. Parks Blvd., Nashville, TN 37228-0988 or e-mailed to permissions@umpublishing.org.

All Scripture quotations, unless otherwise indicated, are taken from the Holy Bible, New International Version®, NIV®. Copyright ©1973, 1978, 1984, 2011 by Biblica, Inc.™ Used by permission of Zondervan. All rights reserved worldwide. www.zondervan.com The "NIV" and "New International Version" are trademarks registered in the United States Patent and Trademark Office by Biblica, Inc.™

Scripture quotations marked (GNT) are from the Good News Translation in Today's English Version, Second Edition © 1992 by American Bible Society. Used by Permission.

ISBN 9781501855313

Manufactured in the United States of America

18 19 20 21 22 23 24 25 26 27—10 9 8 7 6 5 4 3 2 1

ABINGDON PRESS
Nashville

TABLE OF CONTENTS

1. Entering the Promised Land (Joshua 1–3) 7
2. The Battle of Jericho (Joshua 4–6) 16
3. The Sin of Achan (Joshua 7–8) 25
4. Joshua Defeats the Kings (Joshua 9–12) 32
5. Joshua Divides the Territory (Joshua 13–17) 42
6. Seven Portions Remain (Joshua 18–21) 50
7. Joshua Prepares to Die (Joshua 22–24) 58
8. The Lord Raised Up Judges (Judges 1–3) 67
9. Deborah and Gideon (Judges 4–8) 75
10. Abimelek and Jephthah (Judges 9–12) 83
11. Samson the Nazirite (Judges 13–16) 91
12. Micah and the Danites (Judges 17–21) 100
13. The Story of Ruth (Ruth 1–4) 109
Glossary of Terms 117

"Get ready to cross the Jordan River into the land I am about to give to . . . the Israelites." (1:2)

1

ENTERING THE PROMISED LAND

Joshua 1–3

DIMENSION ONE: WHAT DOES THE BIBLE SAY?

Answer these questions by reading Joshua 1

1. Who takes over the leadership of Israel when Moses dies? (Joshua 1:1-2)

2. What part of the land the Israelites are about to enter will God give to them? (Joshua 1:3)

3. What does the Lord promise to Joshua? (Joshua 1:5, 9)

4. What condition does God lay down for the success of the coming conquest? (Joshua 1:7)

5. What is Joshua to do with the Book of the Law? (Joshua 1:8)

6. What does Joshua order the Reubenites, the Gadites, and the half-tribe of Manasseh to do? (Joshua 1:12-15)

7. How do these tribes respond to Joshua's command? (Joshua 1:16-17)

Answer these questions by reading Joshua 2

8. Where do the two spies go? (Joshua 2:1)

9. How does Rahab reply to the king of Jericho's command to turn over the two men? (Joshua 2:4-5)

10. Where are the two spies? (Joshua 2:6)

11. What does Rahab request of the two Israelite men? (Joshua 2:12-13)

12. How do the two men respond to Rahab's request? (Joshua 2:14)

13. What sign do the spies tell Rahab to display in order to save her family from death? (Joshua 2:18)

14. What do the spies report to Joshua? (Joshua 2:24)

ENTERING THE PROMISED LAND

Answer these questions by reading Joshua 3

15. What will lead the Israelites into the Promised Land? (Joshua 3:3)

16. How do the people prepare to cross the Jordan River? (Joshua 3:5)

17. Where does Joshua say the living God will be? (Joshua 3:10)

18. Joshua says the waters will stop flowing when? (Joshua 3:13)

19. What time of year does Israel cross the Jordan? (Joshua 3:15)

20. Where is the ark of the covenant while the people pass over the Jordan on dry ground? (Joshua 3:17)

DIMENSION TWO: WHAT DOES THE BIBLE MEAN?

■ **Joshua 1:1.** In this verse, God speaks to Joshua for the first time. Joshua's name means "Yahweh is salvation," and appears elsewhere in the Bible in the forms *Hosea* and *Jesus* (see Matthew 1:21). Israelite names often contained faith statements about God. Joshua's name was one of the first to use the divine name revealed to Moses (see Exodus 3:14-15).

- **Joshua 1:4.** God tells Joshua that the Promised Land will include all the area found between the deserts to the east and south, the Mediterranean Sea to the west, the Lebanon mountains to the northwest, and the Euphrates River to the northeast. While Israel never controlled all this land, it did approach these borders later under the reign of King David.
- **Joshua 1:7-8.** The "Book of the Law" refers to the Book of Deuteronomy. These verses continue the understanding that by following the written law the Israelites are guaranteed success.
- **Joshua 1:12-18.** Joshua tells the tribes of Reuben, Gad, and the half-tribe of Manasseh that they will receive territory east of the Jordan River (see Numbers 32; Deuteronomy 3:12-20). Still, they join with the other tribes to conquer the land west of the river. Joshua emphasizes that all Israel should be one people united in action under one God.
- **Joshua 2:1.** Shittim is an area about seven miles east of the Jordan River. Jericho stands about five miles west of the river and seven miles north of the Dead Sea. At Jericho is a spring capable of watering thousands of acres. Already in Joshua's day (about 1250–1225 BC), Jericho had been occupied off and on for almost seven thousand years.

The prostitute Rahab's name means "wide" or "broad." Apparently the men go to her place of business to escape detection. The idea of strangers visiting a prostitute is not unusual. However, their scheme does not work.

According to Matthew 1:5, Rahab is one of Jesus' ancestors.
- **Joshua 2:2-5.** Rahab tells the king's agents that the men were with her only briefly and that they left the city before dark. Ancient cities closed their gates at night so they could not be attacked and captured under the cover of darkness.
- **Joshua 2:6.** Rahab not only lies to the king's men; she also hides the Israelite spies under flax drying on her roof. Flax, used in making linen, is harvested in the spring.

■ **Joshua 2:9-11.** Here Rahab gives an Israelite confession of faith. It shares much in common with similar confessions found in Deuteronomy (see Deuteronomy 26:5-10). A native of the land and a prostitute, she now places her trust in Yahweh, Israel's God.

Rahab's confession contains several important themes that we will find again in the holy war tradition in Joshua. These holy wars will be won, not by what Israel does, but by what God does. The people of Canaan will lose because God has already put the fear of Israel upon them, and they "melted in fear" (v. 11) before Israel. The statement on the Red Sea in verse 10 differs, interestingly, from the Exodus version. Rahab says God "dried up the water"; Exodus 14:21 states the waters were blown back and divided.

■ **Joshua 2:12-14.** Rahab requests that the Israelites return the kind deed she has done for the spies. As she has hidden the spies and lied to her king to save their lives, she asks that they promise to save her and her family. This appeal looks forward to the element of Israel's wars that poses the most difficulty to modern readers: the total destruction of the defeated people. (The next lesson will deal more fully with this issue). Here, however, the Israelite spies promise to save her life.

■ **Joshua 2:15.** Apparently, Rahab's house is built right into the city wall. She now performs a third kindness for the spies. She helps them escape the trap of the closed city.

■ **Joshua 2:18-21.** The spies tell Rahab to mark her location with a scarlet cord. This sign will enable them to save her family from death. The color of the cord reminds us of the blood on the doorposts during the first Passover (see Exodus 12:13).

■ **Joshua 2:24.** The spies do not report military information. Rather, they affirm that God has already accomplished the promise of land. The natives fear Israel and God. The land is already theirs.

■ **Joshua 3:3-4.** The ark of the covenant (see Exodus 25:10-22) is the central symbol of God's presence in war. The ark is a sort of war throne from which Yahweh leads the people to victory (see Numbers 10:35-36). Yahweh's power literally radiates from this throne. Consequently, only Levites—specially chosen by God for the task—can touch the ark. Ordinary people must keep a safe distance. We see the dangerous potential of the ark's power upon ordinary people in the story of Uzzah's death for steadying the ark (see 2 Samuel 6:6-7).

■ **Joshua 3:5.** The crossing of the Jordan is a sacred occasion that follows a pattern of religious worship. Before the people can witness God's actions or worship God, they must first prepare themselves. This sanctifying process involves consciously redirecting their thoughts from everyday concerns to those of God. Israelites did this by washing their bodies and clothes (see Exodus 19:10-11) and cleaning the camp (see Deuteronomy 23:9-14). This practice of preparation before standing in God's presence is another emphasis in the holy war tradition.

■ **Joshua 3:9.** Here begins a solemn sermon that again signals to us the religious and ritual nature of the crossing of the Jordan.

■ **Joshua 3:10.** This list of natives living in the Promised Land shows that the land has seen many migrations and conquests before Joshua's time. This list witnesses to the mixed population Israel meets as it moves into its God-granted territory.

■ **Joshua 3:13.** Joshua tells the people ahead of time what will happen. One of the major points of this book is to demonstrate how God announces future deeds ahead of time and then carries out this word in action.

■ **Joshua 3:14-17.** Under Joshua, the new generation born in the desert, which had not experienced the Exodus, now experiences a parallel example of God's power.

■ **Joshua 3:15.** This verse notes that the crossing takes place during spring harvest time when the melting snow from the

ENTERING THE PROMISED LAND

mountains to the north floods the Jordan. For most of the rest of the year, the Jordan remains quite shallow and easily waded. Only in spring would such a miraculous crossing be necessary.

■ **Joshua 3:16.** The waters of the Jordan stop flowing approximately eighteen miles north of Israel's crossing point near Jericho. The wall of water, then, occurs well beyond the sight of the Israelites.

DIMENSION THREE: WHAT DOES THE BIBLE MEAN TO ME?

Joshua 1:1-18—Passing on Leadership

Moses is dead and Israel needs a new leader. Even the great Moses is subject to death. Only God is eternal. No matter how great a leader is, his or her leadership must come to an end and somebody else must take over. But for the new leader to do an effective job, those who are led must accept and follow the new leader. Recognizing that Joshua too serves God, Israel pledges to obey Joshua just as it obeyed Moses.

How often in our lives do we accept and follow a new leader? How do you react when an incumbent politician you like is defeated and a new person takes office? How do you respond to a new pastor when you felt attached to the one leaving? Are you willing, like Israel, to be loyal to God, not to some specific representative of God? How can we maintain what is precious from past leaders yet still accept the need for new and different leadership? How can we distinguish our primary loyalty to God's eternal leadership from our temporary loyalty to God's transitory human representatives?

Joshua 2:1-14—People of Disrepute

A prostitute announces in words and actions her firm faith in Israel's God. For most of us, a prostitute makes an improbable heroine for a biblical story. But when we remember Jacob's trickery, Moses' murder, David's adultery, or Paul's early persecution of Christians, we realize how often the Bible portrays God using disreputable people to accomplish the goal of salvation. Rather than being peopled with saints, the Bible portrays God calling all-too-human persons to do God's will. We will see this theme especially when we look at the Book of Judges.

How do you react to this common biblical portrayal? Why does God so often call on persons that seem irreligious rather than on religious people? Do religious people have some built-in barrier to hearing God? Why did the religious people of Jesus' day reject him, for example, while thieves, prostitutes, and sinners accepted him?

Joshua 3:1-6—Sanctity and Wonders

The Israelites prepare themselves to witness God's power in action. They take very seriously what it means to stand in God's presence. They do not accept God's saving gifts sloppily. They must be prepared to accept God's grace. A large part of witnessing is being prepared to see God's grace first. With expectancy, hope, and preparation they wait on the Lord.

How often do we prepare ourselves to encounter God's grace in our lives? Do we even expect to meet God in church, let alone in our daily lives? How can we direct our thoughts toward God as we go about our work and play? In what ways can we prepare ourselves ahead of time to encounter God in the worship service?

ENTERING THE PROMISED LAND

Joshua 3:7-17—Effects, Not Miracles

Unlike the record of the crossing of the Red Sea in Exodus 14:21-29, here the people see no wall of water. They do not see the miracle directly. They see only its indirect results, the now dry riverbed.

Are we able to see God in the indirect effects of God's work, or do we demand to see God's actions directly? Are we willing to act on the basis of our trust that God leads us, or do we demand proof before we will follow? How is the demand for proof a sign of weak faith? What does it mean to trust and believe in God without seeing?

GENESIS to REVELATION **JOSHUA**

"When the people gave a loud shout, the wall collapsed."
(6:20)

2

THE BATTLE OF JERICHO

Joshua 4–6

DIMENSION ONE: WHAT DOES THE BIBLE SAY?

Answer these questions by reading Joshua 4

1. What does the Lord tell Joshua he wants the twelve men, one from each tribe, to do? (Joshua 4:3)

2. What is the purpose of the stones? (Joshua 4:6-7)

3. What does Joshua set up in the midst of the Jordan? (Joshua 4:9)

4. How do the people feel toward Joshua after the crossing? (Joshua 4:14)

5. What happens after the priests bearing the ark come up out of the riverbed? (Joshua 4:18)

THE BATTLE OF JERICHO

6. Where do the people camp after crossing the Jordan? (Joshua 4:19)

7. Why does Joshua set up the twelve stones? (Joshua 4:20-24)

Answer these questions by reading Joshua 5

8. How do the kings of the Amorites and Canaanites react after they hear about the Israelites crossing the Jordan? (Joshua 5:1)

9. Why does Joshua circumcise all the male Israelites at this time? (Joshua 5:3-5)

10. Why is the place of the Israelite camp called Gilgal? (Joshua 5:9)

11. What religious festival do the Israelites keep at Gilgal? (Joshua 5:10)

12. What happens the day after this festival? (Joshua 5:11-12)

13. Whom does Joshua meet when he is near Jericho? (Joshua 5:13-14)

GENESIS to REVELATION JOSHUA

Answer these questions by reading Joshua 6

14. What does the Lord say to Joshua about Jericho? (Joshua 6:2)

15. What part do the priests play in taking Jericho? (Joshua 6:4)

16. How do the people participate in Jericho's capture? (Joshua 6:5, 20)

17. Where is the ark of the Lord during the march around the city? (Joshua 6:12-13)

18. What does Joshua command the people to do after the seventh circle of Jericho on the seventh day? (Joshua 6:16-17)

19. What does Joshua warn will happen if anyone takes something devoted to destruction? (Joshua 6:18)

20. What do the Israelites do when Jericho's walls fall down flat? (Joshua 6:20-21)

21. Who survives Jericho's fall? (Joshua 6:22-23)

22. How do the Israelites complete their conquest of Jericho? (Joshua 6:24)

THE BATTLE OF JERICHO

23. What curse does Joshua speak over Jericho's ruins? (Joshua 6:26-27)

DIMENSION TWO: WHAT DOES THE BIBLE MEAN?

■ **Joshua 4:2-3.** Here the Lord elaborates on Joshua's command (see 3:12-13) and explains what the twelve men are to do. They shall carry one stone apiece from the riverbed, where the priests stood, to that night's camp. There they will "put them down." Joshua will "set up" the stones (4:20).

■ **Joshua 4:6-7.** Joshua states that the primary reason for taking the stones is to make a memorial specifically for Israel's children. Later in this chapter, the purpose for the memorial will be extended (4:24).

Joshua 4:9. Joshua sets up twelve stones in the Jordan where the priests stood. No reason is given for this act, which is in strange contrast to the two separate explanations given for the twelve stones at Gilgal (4:6-7, 21-24). These stones are still visible when this story was written. Often past events are tied to present scenes visible to readers (see Joshua 6:25; 7:26; 8:28; 10:27).

■ **Joshua 4:10-11.** The Good News Translation (GNT) of the Bible probably best explains the complicated movement in these verses:

> *The priests stood in the middle of the Jordan until everything had been done that the LORD ordered Joshua to tell the people to do. . . . The people hurried across the river. When they were all on the other side, the priests with the LORD's Covenant Box went on ahead of the people.*

■ **Joshua 4:14.** The results of the crossing are interesting. The people now hold Joshua in "awe." The same word is found in the phrase, "the fear of the LORD is the beginning of knowledge" (Proverbs 1:7). The word refers not so much to fright or terror as to reverence, respect, and awe. As God's representative, Joshua receives the reverence due to God.

■ **Joshua 4:19.** We do not know exactly where Gilgal is. Apparently, it lies on the eastern border of the territory of Jericho. We need to remember that the cities in Palestine consist of more than just the buildings within the walls. They are city states that control a large amount of the surrounding land. Gilgal will remain Israel's base of operations throughout the time of conquest.

■ **Joshua 4:21-24.** The explanation Joshua gives for setting up the stones has a different thrust here than the one found in 4:7. In verse 7, the memorial was for Israel only. In these verses, the memorial becomes a sign for not only for Israel, but "all the peoples of the earth" (v. 24).

■ **Joshua 5:3.** Gibeath Haaraloth means "hill of foreskins." Apparently, the hill where the circumcisions are performed is near Gilgal. The law requires that all males who participate in the Passover have to be circumcised (Exodus 12:43-49).

■ **Joshua 5:4-7.** Since, according to Jewish law, all males were to be circumcised when they were eight days old (Genesis 17:10-14), the Israelites would normally already have been circumcised. Since only circumcised men could join in Passover, these verses suggest that Passover has not been celebrated during the years in the desert.

■ **Joshua 5:9.** The "reproach of Egypt" may refer to Israel's original desire, forty years earlier, to return to Egypt after hearing reports of frightening inhabitants in the Promised Land (see Numbers 14:3-4).

■ **Joshua 5:12.** Now that Israel eats the food of the Promised Land, the people no longer need the miraculous manna that kept them alive in the desert. The manna begins immediately after the Israelites cross the Red Sea (Exodus 16) and ends right after they cross the Jordan. We see here another parallel between these two miraculous events.

THE BATTLE OF JERICHO

■ **Joshua 5:13-15.** This story of Joshua's meeting the Lord's commander is similar to the story of Moses at the burning bush (Exodus 3:1-6). God orders both of them to take off their shoes because they are standing on holy ground. Joshua 5:15 asserts the special sanctity of the Promised Land as that which belongs to the Lord. According to the Bible, God's messengers appear in human form, not immediately recognizable as divine (see Genesis 18:1-3; 32:24-30; Judges 13:8-20; Mark 16:1-8).

■ **Joshua 6:1-2.** Verse 1 explains the situation of Jericho and sets the stage for the following words of the Lord. In the Bible, we find no distinction made between the word of God's commander and the word of God. Since the messenger (the commander) speaks God's word directly, to hear the messenger speak is to hear God speak.

■ **Joshua 6:3-5.** Just as with the crossing, God's directions are more religious than military. The conquest will be an act of God that the people will participate in through a ritual. The number seven is sacred to the Jews as the number representing wholeness and perfection (see Genesis 2:2-3).

■ **Joshua 6:15.** All this activity on the seventh day appears strange in light of the commandment against work on the sabbath (see Exodus 20:8-11; Deuteronomy 5:12-15).

■ **Joshua 6:17.** The term *devoted* originally referred to separating the spoils of holy war from all human use by killing all the people and destroying all the goods. Since God won the battle, Israel believes the booty belongs to the Lord and that humans should not reap rewards from war. Although Yahweh uses war to punish the evil inhabitants of the land (see Deuteronomy 9:4-5; 20:16-18); Israel does not deserve to gain from the suffering of the Canaanites.

■ **Joshua 6:18.** Since things devoted to God are sacred and holy, stealing them brings the same danger as touching the ark (see lesson 1, on Joshua 3:3-4).

■ **Joshua 6:22-25.** Joshua remains faithful to the oath the two spies swore to Rahab. He does not kill Rahab or her family. Mercy that is faithful to a promise takes precedence over the literal fulfillment of the law (Deuteronomy 20:16-18). Rahab's descendants apparently continue to live in Israel.

■ **Joshua 6:26.** A curse holds the same importance as a promise. Israel believes that blessings and curses will be fulfilled. Joshua's curse on the rebuilder of Jericho will fall on Hiel of Bethel as told in 1 Kings 16:34.

DIMENSION THREE: WHAT DOES THE BIBLE MEAN TO ME?

Joshua 4:1-7, 19-24—Signaling God's Deeds

Joshua sets up a monument to remind the people of what God has done for them. The monument is a visual sign for all the world of God's power. Whenever people see the stones, God's deeds will remain in their minds.

How do we remember what God has done for us? How do we signal others that God has touched our lives? What kind of memorial can we create to tell our children and others that we have encountered God's grace in our lives? How can we reveal to others we are indeed Christians?

Joshua 5:2-12—Old Signs and New Signs

A new generation of Israelites joins in the old covenant with God by means of circumcision. A relationship with God is not automatic. Each generation must accept the covenant obligations for itself. But each generation's relationship with God is different. The manna, always there during the present generation's life, ends. This generation enters into the old covenant and immediately experiences God's providence differently than ever before. God acts in a new way.

How do we participate in the old covenant today? How can we be open to acts of God that we have not experienced before? How do we know what we should keep from the past and what we should give up? Why does God, while remaining faithful to the old promises, continually act in new ways with the people?

Joshua 6:15-21—Devoted to the Lord

Most modern readers find the idea of holy war, with its total destruction of the enemy people, repulsive. Many people claim that such passages portray God as ruthless. But before we too quickly condemn the ancient Israelites, we should remember that our supposedly modern culture officially ended slavery only in 1865, and has still to give full, equal rights to women and minority groups.

The Israelites believed that by totally destroying the enemy and their goods they could keep from debasing what God had done for them. By devotion of all the spoils of war to God, Israel says that God alone is central to its life. Israel does not follow the Lord for material gain. All that might distract Israel from its loyalty to the Lord must be put aside.

How can we devote ourselves to God alone? Do we believe in God because we think this belief benefits us? Should we trust God even if we see no profit from it? How do we handle those things that compete for our loyalty to God? What should we put under a spiritual ban to ensure that we remain true to God alone?

Joshua 6:21-25—Mercy in the Face of Judgment

We may be repelled by the description of all who die in the fall of Jericho. But the emphasis is not on those who fall in judgment; rather, it is on those who live by mercy—Rahab and her family. As inhabitants of Jericho, they should have died along with the rest, but because of Rahab's trust in God, they were spared and lived with the chosen people.

When do we show mercy to those who, in our eyes, have done wrong? How do we react when someone we consider evil claims to have found God? Do we call for God's judgment on others or for God to show them mercy? How can we recognize the Rahabs around us? How can we, as followers of Christ, show them God's mercy through our actions?

"I have sinned against the LORD, the God of Israel." (7:20)

3
THE SIN OF ACHAN
Joshua 7–8

DIMENSION ONE: WHAT DOES THE BIBLE SAY?

Answer these questions by reading Joshua 7

1. Why does the Lord's anger burn against the people of Israel? (Joshua 7:1)

2. Where does Joshua send the spies? (Joshua 7:2)

3. What do the spies report to Joshua? (Joshua 7:3)

4. What is the outcome of the first attack on Ai? (Joshua 7:4-5)

5. What does Joshua ask the Lord after the attack? (Joshua 7:7-9)

6. How does the Lord answer Joshua? (Joshua 7:11-12)

7. What does the Lord command the Israelites to do the next day? (Joshua 7:13-14)

8. What will happen to the person who has taken devoted things? (Joshua 7:15)

9. Who is identified as the guilty person? (Joshua 7:18)

10. What does Joshua ask Achan to do? (Joshua 7:19)

11. How is Achan punished? (Joshua 7:24-25)

12. What happens after Achan is punished? (Joshua 7:26)

Answer these questions by reading Joshua 8

13. After the punishment, what does the Lord say to Joshua? (Joshua 8:1-2)

14. What does Joshua tell the fighting men to do? (Joshua 8:3-8)

15. How does Joshua signal the moment of ambush? (Joshua 8:18)

16. Why don't the men of Ai flee when they see their city on fire? (Joshua 8:20-21)

THE SIN OF ACHAN

17. How is the ban applied to Ai? (Joshua 8:25-27)

18. What does Joshua do with the king of Ai? (Joshua 8:29)

19. Where does Joshua build an altar to the Lord? (Joshua 8:30)

20. What does Joshua write on the stones of the altar? (Joshua 8:32)

21. Where do the people stand to receive the blessings from the priests? (Joshua 8:33)

22. What does Joshua do in the presence of all the people? (Joshua 8:34)

23. Who hears all the words read by Joshua? (Joshua 8:35)

DIMENSION TWO: WHAT DOES THE BIBLE MEAN?

■ **Joshua 7:1.** Achan's name appears to be related to the word *achar*, meaning "trouble" (see below 7:24, 26; also see 1 Chronicles 2:7). Achan's theft of devoted things breaks Joshua's command found in 6:18. Israel believes that all its members are bound together in covenant with God. What any one person does always affects the group to which he or she belongs. As a result, when Achan breaks the covenant, the whole people become guilty and suffer the consequences.

■ **Joshua 7:2.** Ai stands about one and one half miles east of Bethel. The name *Ai* means "the ruin." Joshua's command to the spies to "go up" to Ai is more than just a conventional phrase. Ai is more than twenty-five hundred feet above sea level, while Jericho lies about eight hundred feet below sea level. *Bethel*, an ancient sanctuary founded by Jacob (see Genesis 28:10-22), means "house of God." Later, a golden bull is worshiped there (see 1 Kings 12:28-30; Hosea 10:5). Faithful worshipers of the Lord nicknamed it *Beth Aven*, which means "house of wickedness." Actually *Bethel* and *Beth Aven* are different names for the same place.

■ **Joshua 7:5.** Achan's sin is responsible for the death of thirty-six men. God turns away from Israel because of Achan's theft. As the small army flees back toward Jericho, they descend into the Jordan valley. This area was called, for obvious reasons, the descent.

■ **Joshua 7:6.** By tearing their clothes and pouring dust on their heads, Joshua and the elders are indicating they are in mourning (see Job 1:20; 2:12).

■ **Joshua 7:7-9.** Joshua's words accuse God of unfaithfulness. They echo words spoken by the Exodus generation when it first heard reports of the inhabitants of the Promised Land (see Deuteronomy 1:27-28).

■ **Joshua 7:14-18.** The process described here involves the use of the sacred lot. In the chance throw of the lot, a sort of dice, Israel believes it can see the will of God. Since the lot is capable of only a yes or no answer, discovering the guilty individual requires a narrowing process. First tribes, then families, then households, and finally individuals go before the lot. Each time marks the guilty group until finally it points to the person responsible.

■ **Joshua 7:22-24.** By placing the items devoted to destruction under his tent, Achan also contaminates his family goods. Now they too must suffer the strictures of the original ban on Jericho and be destroyed.

■ **Joshua 7:25-26.** The valley where the execution and burial occur is named for the trouble Achan brings upon Israel.

THE SIN OF ACHAN

According to Joshua 15:7, the Valley of Achor rests on the later boundary between the tribes of Benjamin and Judah, about five miles south of Jericho.

- **Joshua 8:2.** Here God's way of dealing with the conquest of the Promised Land shifts radically. First, the Lord limits the devotion to destruction of the people alone, which goes against God's earlier commandment in Deuteronomy 20:16-18. Israel may now keep for itself the livestock and spoils. Also, this victory, in contrast to the one in Jericho, occurs by means of a military ambush rather than through ritual actions.
- **Joshua 8:4.** One way the Israelites determine directions is by facing east, which they call front. Left is north, right is south, and behind is west. Thus they are to lie in ambush on the west side of the city.
- **Joshua 8:10-13.** These verses appear to repeat and expand upon verse 9, describing how most of the thirty thousand troops camped north of Ai. A smaller group of five thousand men set up the ambush between Bethel and Ai. Since only a mile and a half separate the two towns, only a small force could remain hidden.
- **Joshua 8:17.** The men of Bethel join the men of Ai in their pursuit of Israel. We do not know how they cross the area between the towns without revealing the ambush (see verse 9). Perhaps this is God's protective action in a story where human action appears to dominate.
- **Joshua 8:18.** The Lord's command to Joshua to raise the javelin in his hand reminds us of Moses' upheld hand that brought Israel victory over Amalek (Exodus 17:8-13).
- **Joshua 8:29.** Ai literally becomes the ruin, and the king of Ai is hanged like a condemned murderer (see Deuteronomy 21:22-23).
- **Joshua 8:30-32.** Suddenly the narrative shifts to the region of Mounts Ebal and Gerizim, twenty miles north of Ai, without any description of how Israel moved into this area. Since the ancient and powerful city of Shechem sits directly in the valley between these two mountains, the ceremony

described here occurs in the vicinity of Shechem. Shechem apparently joins with Israel, without battle or enforcement of the ban. The city will appear in the important covenant ceremony described later in Joshua 24 (see lesson 7).

As soon as Israel's way to the twin mountains (Mount Gerizim and Mount Ebal) is cleared by the fall of Jericho and Ai, Joshua leads the people there to carry out the covenant renewal ceremony commanded by Moses in Deuteronomy 27:4-26. Joshua writes a copy of the Law of Moses on the altar of uncarved stones (see Exodus 20:25) so all the people can see it.

■ **Joshua 8:33-35.** Israel fulfills all Moses commanded it to do and say. Both the blessings and curses spoken in the ceremony are found in Deuteronomy 27:1–28:6. Mount Gerizim, before which half the people stand, symbolizes the blessings God gives those faithful to the covenant. Mount Ebal, before which the other half stand, represents the curses that fall on any who break the covenant. Verse 35 emphasizes that adult males are not the only ones to take on the obligations of God's law; women, children, and aliens resident among the Israelites also participate fully in the covenant bond with God.

DIMENSION THREE: WHAT DOES THE BIBLE MEAN TO ME?

Joshua 7:1-5, 24-26—Evil Affects Others

Achan's sin brings punishment upon his people and his family. Israel believes that what one person does always affects the lives of those around him or her. An evil deed explodes, shattering not only the life of the one who does wrong, but the lives of everyone he or she touches.

How often have you experienced the results of someone else's wrongdoing? Has anyone suffered from something

THE SIN OF ACHAN

you did wrong? How do you deal with this reality? Why is sin never limited to the one committing it? Does good also radiate out, affecting others? How can we make ourselves always conscious that what we say and do has a powerful impact on others?

Joshua 7:6-13—God's Responsibility or Our Own?

Given the experience of defeat, Joshua immediately assumes God has let Israel down. In response, God claims to have kept the covenant. Israel alone shoulders the responsibility for defeat.

Do you ever look for someone else to blame when things go wrong? Why do we seek outside causes for our own discomforts? Are we willing to assume responsibility when things go right? Why then do we refuse so often to accept responsibility for the misfortune that happens to us? How can we learn to recognize and accept responsibility for what we do?

Joshua 8:14-29—Ambushed by God

The king of Ai sees Israel again and assumes he will defeat it as he did before. Building on the king's fixed preconceptions, Israel, under God's guidance, springs an ambush on the king. He loses his city, his people, and his life.

Have any of us ever gotten in trouble because of our preconceptions? Have you ever jumped to a conclusion, believing you saw the whole situation clearly, only to be proven wrong later? Why do we prejudge new situations? How can we keep prejudices from blinding us to new people or new possibilities in our lives? Do we, like the king of Ai, ever misread God's will because we already feel we know it? How can we become receptive to new situations?

GENESIS to REVELATION **JOSHUA**

"These are the kings of the land whom the Israelites had defeated . . . thirty-one kings in all." (12:1, 24)

4

JOSHUA DEFEATS THE KINGS

Joshua 9–12

DIMENSION ONE: WHAT DOES THE BIBLE SAY?

Answer these questions by reading Joshua 9

1. What do the kings in the hill country and the coastlands do? (Joshua 9:1-2)

2. How do the inhabitants of Gibeon act when they hear what Israel did to Jericho and Ai? (Joshua 9:3-6)

3. What do the Gibeonites ask Israel? (Joshua 9:6)

4. How do the Gibeonites trick Israel? (Joshua 9:9-13)

5. How does Israel respond to the Gibeonite request? (Joshua 9:14-15)

JOSHUA DEFEATS THE KINGS

6. Why don't the Israelites kill the Gibeonites when they learn about the trick? (Joshua 9:18-20)

7. How does Joshua curse Gibeon? (Joshua 9:23)

8. How do the Gibeonites explain their deceit? (Joshua 9:24)

Answer these questions by reading Joshua 10

9. What does Adoni-Zedek, king of Jerusalem, do when he hears about Jericho, Ai, and Gibeon? (Joshua 10:1-5)

10. How does Israel respond to Gibeon's call for help? (Joshua 10:7-9)

11. What happens to Adoni-Zedek's army when Joshua's army appears at Gibeon? (Joshua 10:10)

12. What happens as they flee? (Joshua 10:11)

13. How does the Lord mark the day the Amorites are given over to the people of Israel? (Joshua 10:12-14)

14. Where do the five kings go after they are defeated? (Joshua 10:16-18)

15. After slaughtering the enemy soldiers, what does Joshua do to the five captured kings? (Joshua 10:24-26)

16. What are the names of the towns Joshua captures after the battle at Gibeon? (Joshua 10:28-39)

17. What is the outcome of Joshua's campaign in the southern part of the Promised Land? (Joshua 10:40-42)

Answer these questions by reading Joshua 11

18. How do the kings in the northern hill country respond to Joshua's victories in the south? (Joshua 11:4-5)

19. What happens by the Waters of Merom? (Joshua 11:7-9)

20. How is Hazor treated differently from the other northern cities captured by Joshua? (Joshua 11:13)

21. Why does the Lord harden the hearts of the natives of the land? (Joshua 11:20)

22. What is the outcome of all of Joshua's conquests in the Promised Land? (Joshua 11:23)

JOSHUA DEFEATS THE KINGS

Answer these questions by reading Joshua 12

23. How many kings do the people of Israel defeat east of the Jordan? (Joshua 12:2, 4)

24. How many kings do Joshua and the people defeat west of the Jordan? (Joshua 12:24)

DIMENSION TWO: WHAT DOES THE BIBLE MEAN?

■ **Joshua 9:3.** Gibeon is located about twenty miles west of Jericho and seven miles southwest of Ai. At Gibeon, Solomon will pray to God for the gift of wisdom (see 1 Kings 3:4-15).

■ **Joshua 9:4-6.** Israel used cunning to capture Ai in chapter 8. Now in chapter 9, Israel falls victim to a trick played by some natives of the land. Gibeon had heard that Israel was to kill all those living in the land, but could make peace with those outside the land (see also Deuteronomy 20:10-17). The Gibeonites collect worn-out supplies and old food to fool the Israelites into believing they came from a long way off. If they succeed in establishing peace with Israel, Gibeon's safety is guaranteed by Israel's own oath.

■ **Joshua 9:8-11.** Gibeon offers to enter into a covenant in which Israel will dominate them. By saying "We are your servants" (v. 8), the Gibeonites place themselves under Israelite control and protection. If Israel accepts Gibeon's offer of servanthood, it is obligated by the covenant to protect the Gibeonites under any circumstances. (On Sihon and Og, see Numbers 21:21-35.)

■ **Joshua 9:12-15.** The group wishing to enter into a covenant provides the food for a meal that the two parties eat together to seal their agreement. By accepting and eating the provisions offered by the Gibeonites, Israel accepts the conditions of the covenant. But Israel gets into trouble by not seeking direction from God.

■ **Joshua 9:17.** The Israelites take three days to travel from Gilgal to Gibeon. Later in Joshua 10:9, they will cover the distance in one night. Gibeon has not acted alone, but also on behalf of three nearby cities. Although the exact location of these cities is not known, the towns are probably within seven miles of Gibeon.

■ **Joshua 9:18-21.** These verses witness to the seriousness of oaths spoken by Israel in the name of the Lord. At Sinai, God commanded, "You shall not misuse the name of the Lord your God, for the Lord will not hold anyone guiltless who misuses his name" (Exodus 20:7; Deuteronomy 5:11). A word once spoken in God's name could not be withdrawn, even if it was based on a lie.

■ **Joshua 9:23.** The Gibeonites do not totally escape the consequences of lying about coming "from a distant country" (9:6). As punishment, Joshua forces them to accept literally their offer to become Israel's servant (9:8). In Hebrew, the word *servant* is the same as the word *slave*. Joshua now declares the Gibeonites "will never be released from service as woodcutters and water carriers." Just as Israel must live by its oath, so too must the Gibeonites follow their word.

■ **Joshua 10:8.** In typical terms, the Lord declares Israel's defense of Gibeon to be a holy war (see Joshua 6:2; 8:1, 18).

■ **Joshua 10:9.** Joshua's army covers the mountainous miles to Gibeon overnight. Perhaps this extremely rapid march witnesses to special physical power held by those under God's direction.

■ **Joshua 10:10.** Panic, or confusion, is one of the main ways the Lord defeats Israel's enemies (see Deuteronomy 7:23; 1 Samuel 5:11). The Israelites then kill their enemies as they try to escape. In the running battle that follows, the army of the five kings first flees west about seven miles and then south for at least seventeen miles.

JOSHUA DEFEATS THE KINGS

■ **Joshua 10:11.** The Lord intervenes a second time by throwing large hailstones on the fleeing enemy to kill them. This verse stresses the image of God as a warrior who actively destroys Israel's enemies. God appears only this one time in the Book of Joshua as the direct, death-dealing agent. We have seen this image before, however, in the story of the crossing of the Red Sea (see Exodus 15:1-19).

■ **Joshua 10:12-13.** Since the natives of the land worshiped the sun and moon, the Lord's power over these bodies stresses the power of Israel's God over the gods of the natives.

The Book of Jashar (*Jashar* means "upright, righteous") was apparently a well-known collection of war poetry. We find this book cited again in 2 Samuel 1:17-27 as the source for David's lament over Saul and Jonathan.

■ **Joshua 10:24-25.** In the ancient Near East, placing one's foot on the neck of a conquered enemy was a symbol of complete victory over that enemy. This image reappears in Psalm 110:1, 1 Corinthians 15:25, and Hebrews 10:12-13.

■ **Joshua 10:28-39.** These verses give a list of cities captured by Joshua in the southern part of the Promised Land. The description of each victory follows the same basic pattern. Interestingly, only three cities of the six listed belong to the five kings who originally attacked Gibeon: Lachish, Eglon, and Hebron. We do not find here a description of the capture of Jerusalem or Jarmuth (but compare 12:10-11). The three cities, independent of the five kings whose destruction we read about here, are Makkedah, Libnah, and Debir. Debir was earlier given as the name of one of the five kings (see 10:3). Although Joshua destroys Gezer's king and army, he apparently does not capture the city (see 16:10; Judges 1:29).

■ **Joshua 10:40-43.** This summary of the southern conquest first describes the natural divisions of the land now under Israelite control. Then it gives the basic borders of this area. Kadesh Barnea lies deep in the southern desert, while Gaza is on the seacoast. Goshen is not the area in Egypt described in Genesis, but probably southeastern Palestine. The region mentioned here is basically the area the tribe of Judah will assume (see 15:1-12).

■ **Joshua 11:1-3.** The scene now shifts to the northern part of the Promised Land. The king of Hazor, a large city nine miles north of the Sea of Galilee, forms a coalition to oppose Israel. The location of the other cities mentioned remains uncertain. "The Arabah south of Kinnereth" (v. 2) refers to the Jordan valley south of the Sea of Galilee. Naphoth Dor lies on the coast about twelve miles south of Mount Carmel. Jabin's name appears again in Judges 4:2.

■ **Joshua 11:4.** This verse tells of Israel's first encounter with horses and chariots during the conquest. Chariots were extremely effective weapons against foot soldiers. For this reason, Israel's troops greatly feared them (see 17:16-18).

■ **Joshua 11:5.** The Waters of Merom are located approximately ten miles northeast of Hazor.

■ **Joshua 11:6.** The Lord promises to give Joshua victory. Israel, however, shall not add chariots to its own armament, since it depends on God for its victories, not on more effective weapons. According to later prophets, dependence on chariots reveals lack of faith in God's power to save the people (see Isaiah 31:1).

■ **Joshua 11:8.** The Israelites pursue their scattered enemies as they fan out over twenty miles to the north and northeast.

■ **Joshua 11:16-18.** This summary of the whole area of conquest first describes the natural divisions of the land and then the extreme southern and northern limits of the conquest. The Negev is the desert south of Palestine. Mount Halak marks the southern limit of the conquest as Baal Gad marks the northern limit. Verse 18 tells us the conquest took much longer than we might assume from the campaign summaries we have just read.

■ **Joshua 11:20.** To harden one's heart means to intentionally turn away from God's will. This rejection can

JOSHUA DEFEATS THE KINGS

be a voluntary human decision and act. However, Israel understands that God ultimately controls everything. The Israelites assume that if the Canaanites oppose Israel, resulting in their own destruction, this opposition serves the Lord's purposes.

- **Joshua 11:21-22.** The Anakites, descendants of Anak, are a legendary race of giants who initially made the Israelites afraid to enter Palestine (see Numbers 13:22-33).
- **Joshua 12:1-6.** This chapter summarizes all of Israel's conquests under Moses and Joshua. For Moses' battles against Sihon and Og, east of the Jordan, see Numbers 21:21-35.
- **Joshua 12:7-24.** These thirty-one kings and their cities were conquered by Joshua west of the Jordan. Fifteen new cities appear on this list for which we have no earlier conquest stories: Ceder, Hormah, Arad, Adullam, Bethel, Tappuah, Hepher, Aphek, Lasharon, Taanach, Megiddo, Kedesh, Jokneam in Carmel, Goyim in Gilgal, and Tirzah.

DIMENSION THREE: WHAT DOES THE BIBLE MEAN TO ME?

Joshua 9:3-15—Being Deceptive

By using cunning, the Gibeonites try to convince Israel they are something they are not, people from a far country. Their deceit succeeds at first, but eventually Israel discovers the lie and reduces Gibeon to slavery. The Gibeonites cannot escape being who they are.

When do you find yourself playing a role, pretending to be someone you are not? Do you ever put on a good front for others? Why do we feel compelled to make others think we are better than we really are? When have you claimed that you would never do what you know you have done? Have you ever acted more religious in public than you do in private? On what occasions? When has another person realized that you are not quite the person you project? How can we learn to be more honest about who we are in our relationships with others?

Joshua 9:18-27—Oaths Are for Keeping

Without quite realizing what is involved, Israel takes an oath to protect and defend Gibeon. Israel learns too late just what this commitment means. Ignorance of the whole truth does not excuse the people from keeping the terms of their oath. The Israelites must now live up to the promise so rashly taken.

When have you committed yourself to do something you later found out you did not want to do? When have you made a promise to someone without quite realizing what you were getting into? For example, how many people do you think realize what they are committing themselves to when they say their marriage vows? Similarly, how many people actually understand what it means to promise to submit their lives to God when they join a church? Have you ever wanted to pull back from the full commitment to God that you swore before the altar? What caused you to have such a feeling? What does it mean to become a Christian without quite realizing how totally God claims our lives? How can we truly live up to our oaths to God to love and follow our Lord?

Joshua 10:1-5—Attacking the Wrong Problem

In response to the fall of Jericho and Ai and the surrender of Gibeon, the king of Jerusalem forms a coalition to attack Gibeon. The real threat, of course, comes from Israel. The five kings fear Israel. Consequently, they assault that which poses no real threat to them.

When have you been guilty of attacking a secondary problem to avoid dealing with a major problem? For example, have you ever found yourself picking at the small faults of another person, all the while avoiding the real problems in your relationship with him or her? Why do we try to avoid or put off dealing with the real problems we have with other people? Do you feel people in the church deal adequately with the real problems the world faces? Do we simply treat symptoms rather than root causes of society's ills? How can we keep ourselves from being sidetracked into matters that do not answer the problem at hand? How can we, as church members, ensure that we realistically deal with the causes of our major personal and social problems?

GENESIS to REVELATION **JOSHUA**

"Be sure to allocate this land to Israel for an inheritance."
(13:6)

5

JOSHUA DIVIDES THE TERRITORY

Joshua 13–17

DIMENSION ONE: WHAT DOES THE BIBLE SAY?

Answer these questions by reading Joshua 13

1. What does the Lord say to Joshua? (Joshua 13:1)

2. What does God command Joshua to do? (Joshua 13:6-7)

3. Which tribes receive land east of the Jordan? (Joshua 13:8)

4. Within each tribe, how is the inheritance divided? (Joshua 13:15, 24, 29)

JOSHUA DIVIDES THE TERRITORY

Answer these questions by reading Joshua 14

5. Who distributes the inheritance of the land west of the Jordan? (Joshua 14:1)

6. How is this distribution of the land made for the nine and one half tribes? (Joshua 14:2)

7. Into how many tribes are "Joseph's descendants" divided? (Joshua 14:4)

8. What happens when the men of Judah come to Joshua? (Joshua 14:6-8)

9. What had Moses sworn to Caleb? (Joshua 14:9)

10. How many years have passed since Moses spoke the Lord's word to Caleb? (Joshua 14:10)

11. What land does Caleb receive for his faithfulness? (Joshua 14:13-15)

Answer these questions by reading Joshua 15

12. What does Caleb offer to any one who captures Kiriath Sepher? (Joshua 15:16)

GENESIS to REVELATION JOSHUA

13. Who captures Kiriath Sepher? (Joshua 15:17)

14. What does Caleb's daughter ask of him? (Joshua 15:19)

15. Who are the people of Judah unable to drive out? (Joshua 15:63)

Answer this question by reading Joshua 16

16. Who is the tribe of Ephraim unable to drive out? (Joshua 16:10)

Answer these questions by reading Joshua 17

17. What happens to the daughters of Zelophehad during the distribution of the land? (Joshua 17:3-4)

18. What are the sons of Manasseh unable to do? (Joshua 17:12)

19. What do the people of Joseph ask Joshua? (Joshua 17:14)

20. How does Joshua respond to the question of Joseph's people? (Joshua 17:15)

21. What keeps the people of Joseph from moving beyond the bounds of their original allotment? (Joshua 17:16)

44

22. How does Joshua encourage the house of Joseph? (Joshua 17:17-18)

DIMENSION TWO: WHAT DOES THE BIBLE MEAN?

■ **Joshua 13:1-6.** These verses describe the land not yet in Israel's possession. Although this area is not yet under Israel's control, God commands Joshua to include it in the division of the land. Finding here a list of territory still to be conquered appears strange because Joshua 11:23 stated that "Joshua took the entire land. . . . Then the land had rest from war."

■ **Joshua 13:8-12.** The tribes of Gad, Reuben, and the half-tribe of Manasseh have already been assigned land east of the Jordan by Moses, but they also participate in the conquest of the land west of the Jordan (see Joshua 1:12-17; 4:12). Now that the conquest is over, they officially receive their land.

■ **Joshua 13:14.** The inheritance of the tribe of Levi will be described in chapter 21.

■ **Joshua 13:22.** We read about Israel's encounter with Balaam in Numbers 22–24.

■ **Joshua 14:1.** Eleazar the priest is the son of Moses' brother, Aaron (see Exodus 6:25; Leviticus 10:6; Numbers 3:2). The high priest carries the lot and administers it. Perhaps this is why Eleazar's name precedes Joshua's here.

■ **Joshua 14:2.** See lesson 3 on Joshua 7:14-18 to review the use of the lot in Israel. Israel's belief in the validity of the lot is reflected in Proverbs 16:33: "The lot is cast into the lap, / but its every decision is from the LORD."

■ **Joshua 14:6.** *Caleb* means "dog." To the Israelites, dogs are scavengers, not household pets, so this is not an honorable name. Here we are told that Caleb is not an Israelite, but a Kenizzite (see also Numbers 32:12).

- **Joshua 14:7-9.** Caleb refers to the spy mission described in Numbers 13–14 and Deuteronomy 1:22-28.
- **Joshua 14:10.** Caleb says it has been forty-five years since Moses spoke these words to him. According to Deuteronomy 2:14, Israel wandered for thirty-eight years after leaving Kadesh Barnea. This suggests that the conquest recounted so far in Joshua has taken seven years.
- **Joshua 14:14.** Hebron lies nineteen miles south of Jerusalem, and its capture is described in Joshua 10:36-37. Hebron will later be the capital of the tribe of Judah, where David will reign as king over Judah (see 2 Samuel 2:1-4; 5:1-5).
- **Joshua 15:1.** Judah is the first tribe to receive its allotment of land.
- **Joshua 15:15.** *Kiriath Sepher* means "city of the book." This city may be a training center for scribes or a publishing center for books.
- **Joshua 15:16-17.** Othniel reveals his military prowess by capturing a city to win a wife. Later, after Joshua dies, Othniel will become the first judge over Israel (see Judges 3:7-11, lesson 8).
- **Joshua 15:18.** This verse is extremely difficult to translate. The Hebrew text says "she urged him to ask," but then Aksah immediately asks herself. Consequently, some translations suggest we should read "he urged her."
- **Joshua 15:20-32.** Although the concluding passage of this list of cities gives their number as twenty-nine, the list contains thirty-six names. To explain this discrepancy, one commentator suggests that new lists were inserted as the political situation changed, while the total number was not adjusted accordingly.
- **Joshua 15:63.** Judges 1:8 recounts a conquest of Jerusalem by the tribe of Judah, but in Second Samuel 5:6-9, David receives credit for Jerusalem's capture.
- **Joshua 16:1-3.** The borders for the inheritance of the tribes that descended from Joseph are given in much less detail than are the borders of Judah's land (see Joshua 15:1-12).

■ **Joshua 16:4.** The descendants of Joseph are so numerous that they have been divided into two tribes, named after Joseph's two sons (see Genesis 41:51-52).

■ **Joshua 17:3-6.** Zelophehad, a descendant of Manasseh, had only daughters. According to Israelite custom, they would not inherit anything from their father. In Numbers 27:1-11, Zelophehad's daughters bring their situation to Moses, and the Lord tells him, "If a man dies and leaves no son, turn his inheritance over to his daughter." In our passage from Joshua, these five daughters now come forward to remind Eleazar and Joshua of the Lord's command. They receive land along with the male descendants of Manasseh.

■ **Joshua 17:14-18.** This action appears to be another version of what we just read about in Joshua 16:1-17:2. The descendants of Joseph demand a larger share of the land. But when Joshua assigns them a larger portion, they fear to take it over because of the Canaanites' superior military power.

DIMENSION THREE: WHAT DOES THE BIBLE MEAN TO ME?

Joshua 14:6-15—Outsiders Before Insiders

Before the land west of the Jordan is divided among the tribes of Israel, an outsider steps forward to receive the first portion. Caleb, a non-Israelite, claims the first portion of the land promised to Israel.

Have you ever seen the person you least expected receive an honor or award? How do members of a group feel when someone who is not a member is rewarded? How did the Pharisees react to Jesus when he opened God's kingdom to the tax collectors, harlots, and sinners? How do we react when someone we do not approve of wants to become part of our church? How do we welcome sinners and outcasts into our midst?

Joshua 15:1-12, 20-61—Pictures of Home

The hills of Judah are described here with its borders and the names of its towns. While for us this section may be dry reading, for its original readers, this passage would have recalled many visual memories of home.

What pictures do you keep of places where you have lived in the past? Do you know anybody who collects old photos of his or her hometown? Why do persons collect such pictures? Why do we look at pictures of buildings that sometimes are no longer standing? Is it because they revive memories of golden pasts for us? Do pictures of old home places evoke sad or painful memories? Or do we remember both the promises and the failures of the past? How does remembering the past help us live better in the present?

Joshua 17:3-6—The Weak Must Remind the Strong

The five daughters of Zelophehad must come forward and remind those in control that they too share God's promise. Although Eleazar and, apparently, Joshua (see Numbers 27:2) were both present when the Lord promised an inheritance to these women, the men had not freely offered to include the women in the allotment of the land. The daughters had to assert their rights before the larger community.

How do we react when a minority group steps forward and insists on its rights? How have the demands of ethnic minorities, women, and persons of various sexual orientations and identities been received by the larger culture? Why are minority groups forced to demand their rights? How has our culture, or even our church, ever ignored or forgotten certain groups?

JOSHUA DIVIDES THE TERRITORY

What obligation do those in control have to listen to those who have little power? Should majorities freely guarantee the rights of minorities? Why or why not? How should the good news of God's love for all people affect our actions toward the powerless? How can the church guarantee that all God's children receive their share of God's promises?

GENESIS to REVELATION **JOSHUA**

"After you have written descriptions of the seven parts of the land . . . I will cast lots for you." (18:6)

6

SEVEN PORTIONS REMAIN

Joshua 18–21

DIMENSION ONE: WHAT DOES THE BIBLE SAY?

Answer these questions by reading Joshua 18

1. Where does the whole congregation of Israel now gather? (Joshua 18:1)

2. How many tribes have yet to receive an inheritance? (Joshua 18:2)

3. What does Joshua ask the Israelites? (Joshua 18:3)

4. What are the three men from each tribe to do? (Joshua 18:4-5)

5. After the report by the tribal representatives, what does Joshua do? (Joshua 18:9-10)

SEVEN PORTIONS REMAIN

6. Where does the lot of the tribe of Benjamin fall? (Joshua 18:11)

Answer these questions by reading Joshua 19

7. Where does the tribe of Simeon receive its inheritance? (Joshua 19:1)

8. Why does the tribe of Simeon receive part of Judah's territory? (Joshua 19:9)

9. Which tribes receive the third, fourth, fifth, and sixth allotments? (Joshua 19:10, 17, 24, 32)

10. What does the tribe of Dan do after failing to capture its territory? (Joshua 19:47)

11. After the distribution of the territories, what do the people of Israel do for Joshua? (Joshua 19:49-50)

Answer these questions by reading Joshua 20

12. What purpose do the cities of refuge serve? (Joshua 20:3)

13. When may a slayer return home? (Joshua 20:6)

GENESIS to REVELATION **JOSHUA**

14. What three cities west of the Jordan does Israel set apart as cities of refuge? (Joshua 20:7)

15. What three cities east of the Jordan does Israel set apart as cities of refuge? (Joshua 20:8)

Answer these questions by reading Joshua 21

16. Why do the heads of the Levites come to Eleazar, Joshua, and the tribal leaders? (Joshua 21:1-3)

17. What are the three groups into which the Levites are divided? (Joshua 21:4, 6, 7)

18. How many towns do the Levites receive? (Joshua 21:41)

19. After the tribes take possession of their land, what does the Lord do for them? (Joshua 21:44)

20. What happens to all the Lord's promises to Israel? (Joshua 21:45)

DIMENSION TWO: WHAT DOES THE BIBLE MEAN?

■ **Joshua 18:1.** Israel now moves about fifteen miles northwest from Gilgal to Shiloh. The allotment of land to the remaining tribes occurs in a new place and by a different method.

SEVEN PORTIONS REMAIN

- **Joshua 18:10.** Joshua alone casts the lots for the portions of land at Shiloh. Earlier, Eleazar the high priest, along with the heads of the tribes, participated in the assignment of land (see the note on Joshua 14:1 in lesson 5).
- **Joshua 18:11.** Benjamin's small territory lies between the larger tribes of Judah and Joseph. The tribe of Benjamin inherits the sites of the earliest victories in the battles at Jericho and Ai.
- **Joshua 18:21-24.** Although this list includes Beth Arabah, according to Joshua 15:61, Beth Arabah belongs to the tribe of Judah.
- **Joshua 18:28.** This list places "the Jebusite city," apparently an ancient name for Jerusalem, in the land of Benjamin. But Joshua 15:63 told us that Jerusalem was never captured from the Jebusites by the Israelites. Elsewhere, David receives credit for capturing Jerusalem (see 2 Samuel 5:6-9).
- **Joshua 19:1.** The tribe of Simeon receives the second portion of land. Although Joshua 18:5 says that Judah will continue in its territory, here we are told Simeon receives its lot in the midst of Judah's inheritance.
- **Joshua 19:2-8.** Most of these cities appear in the city lists of Judah found in Joshua 15.
- **Joshua 19:9.** This verse explains why Simeon received land originally given to Judah. The tribe of Judah had more territory than it needed. Simeon, as a separate tribe, will very quickly be absorbed into the tribe of Judah.
- **Joshua 19:10-16.** With the casting of the third lot, we move to the northern part of the Promised Land. This territory is found between the Sea of Galilee and the Mediterranean Sea. Zebulun's lot falls about halfway between these two bodies of water.
- **Joshua 19:17-23.** The fourth lot falls to Issachar. This land lies between the territories of Zebulun and Manasseh, southeast of the Sea of Galilee.
- **Joshua 19:24-31.** Asher's land, the fifth allotment, takes in the Mediterranean coast west of Zebulun's territory and runs north along the eastern border of Phoenicia.

■ **Joshua 19:32-39.** The sixth lot, which goes to Naphtali, takes in the territory that lies northwest of the Sea of Galilee.

■ **Joshua 19:40-46.** The final lot falls to Dan. This tribe's original allotment lies between Ephraim and Judah, west of Benjamin. Some of these cities are found under Judah's city lists (see Joshua 15:33, 45-46).

■ **Joshua 19:47-48.** Dan ultimately will be unable to maintain control of its allotment. Judges 1:34 tells us that the natives of the land drive Dan back from its territory. The stories of Samson, the Danite (see Judges 13–16, lesson 11), reflect the great pressure the Philistines apply to this tribe. Finally, Dan is forced to migrate to the far northern border of the Promised Land. The story of this migration and how Dan captures new land appears in Judges 18 (see lesson 12).

■ **Joshua 19:49-50.** The last act in the division of the land is God granting Joshua his inheritance. The people of Israel give him the city of Timnath Serah, about twelve miles west-southwest of Shiloh. Since Joshua comes from the tribe of Ephraim, he receives his portion from their land.

■ **Joshua 20:1-3.** These verses mention the cities of refuge. The command given earlier through Moses is found in Numbers 35:9-34 and Deuteronomy 19:1-13.

■ **Joshua 20:4-5.** According to Israelite law, judgment of a crime should take into account the motive behind the act. If someone kills a person unintentionally, he or she should not receive the same punishment as someone who purposely kills another (see Exodus 21:12-14). The city of refuge is a place where the unintentional killer can escape death at the hands of the victim's vengeful kinfolk.

■ **Joshua 20:6.** If found innocent of premeditated murder, the killer remains in the city of refuge until the death of the high priest. Apparently, the high priest's death serves as a kind of sacrifice by which the debt of life owed by the killer to the victim is paid. The high priest's life takes the place of the killer's life as far as the demands of justice are concerned. A life has been given for a life (see Exodus 21:23-24).

SEVEN PORTIONS REMAIN

■ **Joshua 20:7-8.** Shechem and Kiriath Arba are holy places in Israel. Kedesh, which means "holy," is also probably a sacred site. The three cities reappear on the list of levitical cities (see Joshua 21:13, 21, 32). Thus the cities of refuge probably gained their status from the ancient belief that people could seek sanctuary at sacred spots.

■ **Joshua 21:1-3.** The division of the land now reaches its climax with the giving of certain cities to Israel's priests, the Levites. The Book of Joshua has repeatedly looked forward to this most important moment (see 13:14, 33; 14:4; 18:7). The command to which the Levites refer here is found in Numbers 35:1-8.

■ **Joshua 21:4-7.** Levi had three sons, who gave their names to the three clans of Levites: Gershon, Kohath, and Merari (see Exodus 6:16; Numbers 3:14-20). Kohath was Levi's second son. However, the Kohathites gained preeminence over the other levitical clans because Aaron, the one designated as high priest by God, was a descendant of Kohath.

■ **Joshua 21:11-12.** These verses explain how Hebron, the city originally given to Caleb (see 14:13-15), passed to the Levites. The smaller villages and the farmland attached to the city-state of Hebron remain Caleb's. However, the fortified city and the pastureland are now transferred to priestly control.

■ **Joshua 21:44.** "Rest" is the goal that Israel has repeatedly sought (see Deuteronomy 12:10; Joshua 1:13, 15; 11:23; 23:1). Rest is the experience of peace, security, and prosperity in the land given by the Lord.

DIMENSION THREE: WHAT DOES THE BIBLE MEAN TO ME?

Joshua 20:1-6—Judge the Motive, Not the Act

If a person kills another unwittingly, Israel believes he or she should not receive the same punishment as one who kills intentionally. What is judged here is not the act itself, but the reason behind the act. Israel believes that God is more concerned with the inward motive than with the outward act.

How do we judge others? When do you try to discover motives behind persons' actions? Can you always tell why someone did something by just looking at the deed? Do good actions always imply good motives? What did Jesus mean when he told us not to judge others (see Matthew 7:1)?

When have you been judged wrongly? When have you found yourself doing what appears to be right, but for the wrong reason, like giving a compliment you didn't really mean or helping somebody you didn't want to help? When have you done something you knew others would judge negatively, but felt you still had to do, like helping someone others disapprove of or breaking a law to help a friend? How can we discover the reasons why people act the way they do? How can we learn to understand the motives of others?

Joshua 21:1-3—God's Servants Deserve a Portion

The Levites come forward, like Caleb and the daughters of Zelophehad, to remind the people that, by God's command, they too deserve a share of the Promised Land. By giving them some of the best cities, Israel affirms that those who serve God should receive a generous portion of that which God gives the people.

How do you feel about making sure those who serve God live satisfactorily? What does the pastor deserve from his or her congregation by way of compensation? Does the salary and parsonage, or housing allowance that you give your pastor truly meet his or her needs? How much sacrifice do we require from our pastors and their families? How should we in the church understand Jesus' statement (made as he sent his disciples out to preach), "the worker deserves his wages"? (see Luke 10:7; 1 Corinthians 9:14). How can we ensure that our pastors receive a just reward for the services they give?

Joshua 21:43-45—Rest Is an Active State

Israel achieves rest. The conquest is over. Peace has come. The people possess the land that God promised to their ancestors. All of God's good promises have come to pass. However, rest is not an end; it's a beginning. Rest means that Israel may now begin to live in faithfulness to the Lord in the land God has given it.

How do we see rest? Do we view this concept differently than Israel did? When do we see rest occurring in our lives? Is it something we experience now, or is it something in the future? Do we know rest in this life, or is it something we will encounter beyond this life? How does rest figure in your life of faith? Do you feel at rest in your faith, secure in your relationship with God? Why does the author of Hebrews tells us to "make every effort to enter that rest" (Hebrews 4:11)? How can we use the rest given us by God as a means of living faithfully with God?

"On that day Joshua made a covenant for the people." (24:25)

7

JOSHUA PREPARES TO DIE

Joshua 22–24

DIMENSION ONE: WHAT DOES THE BIBLE SAY?

Answer these questions by reading Joshua 22

1. What does Joshua tell the tribes of Reuben, Gad, and the half-tribe of Manasseh? (Joshua 22:4-5)

2. What do these tribes do when they reach the region around the Jordan? (Joshua 22:10)

3. How do the people of Israel react to the news of what these tribes have done? (Joshua 22:12)

4. Who does Israel send to the land of Gilead? (Joshua 22:13-14)

5. What do these representatives accuse the eastern tribes of doing? (Joshua 22:16)

JOSHUA PREPARES TO DIE

6. How do the Reubenites, the Gadites, and the half-tribe of Manasseh answer the charges against them? (Joshua 22:22-23)

7. What reason do these eastern tribes give for building the altar? (Joshua 22:25-27)

8. How do the representatives of Israel respond to the words of the eastern tribes? (Joshua 22:30-31)

Answer these questions by reading Joshua 23

9. What does Joshua tell Israel that God will do to the nations remaining in its midst? (Joshua 23:5)

10. In response to what God will do for Israel, what does Joshua command Israel to do? (Joshua 23:6)

11. What will happen if the Israelites turn back from God and join the nations left among them? (Joshua 23:12-13)

Answer these questions by reading Joshua 24

12. Where does Joshua assemble all the tribes of Israel? (Joshua 24:1)

13. What does the Lord say concerning their ancestors? (Joshua 24:2)

GENESIS to REVELATION **JOSHUA**

14. What did God do to Abraham? (Joshua 24:3)

15. What happened at the sea when God brought Israel out of Egypt? (Joshua 24:6-7)

16. What does the Lord say happened at Jericho? (Joshua 24:11)

17. What did God send before Israel to drive out the inhabitants of the land? (Joshua 24:12)

18. In light of what God has done for Israel, what does Joshua command the people to do? (Joshua 24:14)

19. No matter what Israel chooses, what does Joshua vow he will do? (Joshua 24:15)

20. How do the people respond to Joshua's command? (Joshua 24:16-18)

21. Does Joshua believe that the people will serve the Lord? (Joshua 24:19)

22. After the people affirm their loyalty a third time, what does Joshua do? (Joshua 24:25-27)

JOSHUA PREPARES TO DIE

23. How old is Joshua when he dies? (Joshua 24:29)

24. How long does Israel serve the Lord? (Joshua 24:31)

25. Who is buried at Shechem by the people of Israel? (Joshua 24:32)

DIMENSION TWO: WHAT DOES THE BIBLE MEAN?

■ **Joshua 22:14.** The tribes of Reuben, Gad, and the half-tribe of Manasseh had received their inheritances from Moses east of the Jordan River (see Numbers 32; Deuteronomy 3:18-20). They still participated in the conquest of the Promised Land (see Joshua 1:12-18). With the completion of the conquest, Joshua now sends them home.
■ **Joshua 22:5.** Here Joshua repeats Deuteronomy's injunction to "love the Lord your God" (see Deuteronomy 6:5).
■ **Joshua 22:10-11.** The western tribes assume, when they hear about the giant altar, that the eastern tribes have broken the Israelite law against having more than one sanctuary and one altar (see Deuteronomy 12:10-14).
■ **Joshua 22:12.** This verse tells us that the whole assembly of Israel gathered. However, from the appointment of ten representatives, one from each tribe (see v. 14), it is obvious that only the nine-and-one-half tribes west of the Jordan are included in this gathering.
■ **Joshua 22:13.** The name *Phinehas* means "the southerner," someone from the south of Egypt. He is the grandson of Moses' brother Aaron, and first appears in Numbers 25:6-13, where he kills a renegade Israelite man and wife. Now he

61

GENESIS to REVELATION: JOSHUA

leads a delegation to investigate the possible apostasy of the eastern tribes.

■ **Joshua 22:17.** Here the people recall the "sin of Peor" from which they have not yet been cleansed. On the events at Peor, see Numbers 25:1-5 and Deuteronomy 4:3.

■ **Joshua 22:19.** This verse suggests that the western tribes did not consider the land of the tribes of Reuben, Gad, and Manasseh to be within the boundaries of the Promised Land. The land east of the Jordan is "defiled."

■ **Joshua 22:20.** On Achan's sin and its consequences for all Israel, see Joshua 7, lesson 3.

■ **Joshua 22:22.** The eastern tribes respond to the charge against them with a statement about God. "Mighty One" translates the patriarchal name for God, *El* (see Genesis 17:1). God is the general Hebrew word for the deity (as used in Genesis 1), while *the* LORD translates God's personal name (see Exodus 3:13-15). The eastern tribes swear their allegiance by all of the ways God has acted on behalf of Israel and its ancestors.

■ **Joshua 22:24-28.** The building of the altar has given rise to that which it was supposed to avert. The altar was supposed to witness that the eastern tribes were part of an Israel united in service to the Lord. However, in building the altar, the eastern tribes of Reuben, Gad, and Manasseh are thought to be severing themselves from the Lord and Israel.

■ **Joshua 22:29.** The eastern tribes reaffirm what their service in the conquest of the Promised Land should have shown—their loyalty to the Lord.

■ **Joshua 23:1-2.** Here, a long time after the division of the land, Joshua appears "a very old man." Much earlier, before the land division, we were told that "Joshua had grown old" (see Joshua 13:1).

The passage does not tell us where Joshua assembles Israel. From what comes before, we might assume this gathering occurs in Shiloh. But in the following chapter,

JOSHUA PREPARES TO DIE

Joshua calls the people to Shechem (see Joshua 24:1). Since chapter 24 is Joshua's testament to Israel, perhaps the people gathered at Joshua's home in Timnath Serah.

■ **Joshua 23:5-6.** Here Joshua states the positive part of God's promise. The Lord will drive out the nations still remaining in Israel's midst, if Israel stays loyal to God by following the laws of Moses.

■ **Joshua 23:12-13.** Joshua now declares the negative part of God's promise. If Israel turns away from the Lord and joins with the nations, God will not drive out these nations, and Israel will perish from the land.

■ **Joshua 23:14-16.** In these verses, Joshua affirms that God will keep either the positive promise or the negative one, depending on Israel's faithfulness.

■ **Joshua 24:2.** By using the phrase "this is what the LORD, the God of Israel, says" Joshua indicates that he is speaking as a prophet (see, e.g., Amos 1:3, 6, 9). On Terah, Abraham, and Nahor, see Genesis 11:27-32.

■ **Joshua 24:7-8.** Note that this summary of God's acts on Israel's behalf does not include the giving of the law at Mount Sinai. (Compare similar summaries in Deuteronomy 6:20-25; 26:5-10). The emphasis in Joshua 24 is on the exodus from Egypt.

■ **Joshua 24:9-10.** On Balak, king of Moab, and his attempt to have Balaam curse Israel, see Numbers 22-24.

The statement in verse 11, that the men of Jericho fought against Israel, contrasts with the account we read in Joshua 6. There the inhabitants of Jericho cowered in fear behind their walls. God caused the walls to fall, and the Israelites slaughtered all but Rahab's family. Nowhere in chapter 6 did we see any active opposition to Israel's attack. These different versions of the same event result from different traditions, each with its own particular emphasis.

■ **Joshua 24:12.** The "hornet" appears to be a metaphor for the panic, terror, and helplessness that God inflicts on Israel's enemies during the holy war (see Joshua 2:11;

GENESIS to REVELATION   JOSHUA

10:1-2). We find this use of *hornet* also in Exodus 23:28 and Deuteronomy 7:20.

■ **Joshua 24:14-15.** Here, for the first time in the Bible, we hear that the Israelites worshiped other gods while they were enslaved in Egypt. Joshua's demand that Israel choose to either serve the old gods or worship the Lord was quite radical. In the culture of that time, all people but the Israelites assumed that a person could worship any number of gods.

■ **Joshua 24:19-20.** The Lord refuses to share Israel's service and loyalty with any other gods. As God shows loyalty to the chosen people, so the Lord expects loyalty in return (see Exodus 20:4-6). Refusal to be faithful to the Lord calls down judgment on the offender.

■ **Joshua 24:25.** In the Bible, Shechem has strong connections with covenant-making traditions. Earlier, Joshua renewed Israel's covenant with the Lord here (see Joshua 8:30-35, lesson 3). We learn later, in Judges 8:33, that Shechem's residents worshiped Baal-Berith, whose name means "lord of the covenant."

■ **Joshua 24:32.** This verse reports that the people bury Joseph's bones in Shechem. Israel finally fulfills Joseph's request that he be buried in the Promised Land (see Genesis 50:24-25).

DIMENSION THREE: WHAT DOES THE BIBLE MEAN TO ME?

Joshua 22:10-14—Excluding the Affected Party

The western tribes hear about an act by the eastern tribes of which they do not approve, the building of an altar. They immediately call together all of Israel. However, they exclude from their deliberation the part of Israel that has caused the problem and could justify its actions. By not inviting the eastern tribes to the assembly, the western

JOSHUA PREPARES TO DIE

tribes learn almost too late that they have misunderstood the actions of the other tribes.

Think of examples where someone has been excluded from a group without knowing why. When have you been involved in a secret meeting to discuss what to do with an erring sister or brother? Why are groups so often afraid to confront directly problems that occur within the group? How do we in the church deal with difficult situations? When we find ourselves working behind the backs of those with whom we disagree, is this a Christian way to face potential conflict? How did Jesus deal with those opposing his views? How can we in the church learn to deal openly and directly with problems and conflicts that inevitably arise?

Joshua 22:21-29—Misinterpreting Others' Actions

The tribes of Reuben, Gad, and the half-tribe of Manasseh built an altar to witness to succeeding generations their unity with the western tribes. However, building the altar had contrary results. The western tribes concluded that the eastern tribes were rebelling against God and the rest of Israel. So that which was built to symbolize unity actually creates disunity.

When have you tried to do something for someone else, only to have your motives misinterpreted? Why do persons raise doubts about what you say and do? Do our actions make persons turn away from Christianity, rather than come to Christianity? How can we in the church avoid turning away the people we are trying to bring in? How can we reveal to persons our active concern for them?

Joshua 23:5-13—God's Positive and Negative Promises

The Lord promises to continue to drive out the inhabitants of the land before the Israelites. This promise depends on Israel's continued loyalty to God. If Israel turns away from the Lord and joins with the people in its midst, God promises that Israel will vanish from the land. Faithfulness to God brings blessing upon Israel; turning away from God results in separation from God. Israel will lose its intimate relationship with the Lord. God makes both promises. Israel must now decide on its own which promise it wants God to fulfill.

What are God's positive and negative promises to us? Who is responsible for deciding which promises we receive? Does God judge us, or do we really judge ourselves? How do persons show that they are rejecting the Lord? How do persons show that they love God and are loyal to God?

Joshua 24:19-24—Can We Serve a Jealous God?

Joshua doubts that Israel can truly serve the Lord. The Lord is a jealous God who refuses to share the people with any other gods. Those who promise to serve the Lord must realize that God will not forgive them for breaking their vow of absolute loyalty. Joshua questions whether the people of Israel can remain totally faithful to the Lord.

Does God have the right to demand absolute loyalty from us? Why or why not? When do we put other loyalties ahead of our loyalty to God? Do we, for example, put family, nation, or even church ahead of God in our lives? When have you had to choose between God and someone or something else? What did you choose? Why? What problems are involved in serving a God who jealously demands your first and total loyalty? Was Joshua right? Or can we meet such a demand?

"The Israelites did evil in the eyes of the LORD." (3:7)

8

THE LORD RAISED UP JUDGES

Judges 1–3

DIMENSION ONE: WHAT DOES THE BIBLE SAY?

Answers these questions by reading Judges 1

1. What happens when Joshua dies? (Judges 1:1-2)

2. What kind of agreement do Judah and Simeon have? (Judges 1:3)

3. What do Judah and Simeon do to Adoni-Bezek when they capture him? (Judges 1:6)

4. What happens when the men of Judah fight against Jerusalem? (Judges 1:8)

5. How successful is Judah in taking the allotted territory? (Judges 1:19)

GENESIS to REVELATION **JUDGES**

6. Who are the people of Benjamin unable to drive out from their land? (Judges 1:21)

7. What other tribes are unable to drive out all the inhabitants of their territories? (Judges 1:27, 29, 30, 31, 33, 34)

Answer these questions by reading Judges 2

8. How does the angel of the Lord explain Israel's failure to capture all the land? (Judges 2:1-3)

9. What do the Israelites do after hearing the angel's message? (Judges 2:4)

10. What happens after the death of the generation that had experienced the conquest? (Judges 2:10)

11. Which gods do the people of Israel serve when they turn away from the Lord? (Judges 2:13)

12. How does God respond to the people's rejection? (Judges 2:14-15)

13. After God punishes Israel for a time, what happens? (Judges 2:16)

THE LORD RAISED UP JUDGES

14. Why does God still act to save the sinful people? (Judges 2:18)

15. What happens when a judge raised up by God dies? (Judges 2:19)

Answer these questions by reading Judges 3

16. What nations does the Lord leave in the land to test the Israelites? (Judges 3:3)

17. What happens when the Lord's anger burns against Israel? (Judges 3:8)

18. Who does God raise up as a deliverer for Israel? (Judges 3:9)

19. What happens when Israel's first deliverer dies? (Judges 3:12)

20. How is Ehud different from other people? (Judges 3:15)

21. How does Ehud prepare himself to meet the Moabite king? (Judges 3:16)

22. What message from God does Ehud deliver to Eglon? (Judges 3:20-22)

GENESIS to REVELATION **JUDGES**

23. What does Ehud do after his escape? (Judges 3:27-28)

24. Who kills six hundred Philistines with an oxgoad? (Judges 3:31)

DIMENSION TWO: WHAT DOES THE BIBLE MEAN?

■ **Judges 1:1-3.** Unlike what happened when Moses dies, God does not appoint anyone to lead Israel upon Joshua's death. The people ask God who should lead them, and God designates the whole tribe of Judah. But instead of uniting all Israel behind its leadership, Judah joins only with Simeon to capture its own land. With Joshua's death, unified tribal actions disappear.

■ **Judges 1:5-6.** *Adoni-Bezek* means "Lord of Bezek" and is more a title than a name. Cutting off the thumbs and big toes of a captured enemy keeps him from ever taking up weapons again.

■ **Judges 1:8.** This verse disagrees with Joshua 15:63, which states Judah was unable to capture Jerusalem. Judges 1:21 states that Benjamin also fails to take Jerusalem.

■ **Judges 1:16.** "The City of Palms" is another name for Jericho (see 3:13).

■ **Judges 1:18.** These cities are part of the five-city Philistine confederation. This verse contrasts with the suggestion in Judges 3:3 that the Philistines were not conquered.

■ **Judges 1:22-26.** Although Bethel is closely allied with Ai (see Joshua 7:2; 8:17), its capture apparently does not occur until much later than that of Ai. Luz, the name given by the traitor to his new city, appropriately means "deception."

■ **Judges 1:27-36.** This list of land the tribes have not captured has sometimes been called the account of the Negative Conquest. The lack of success on the part of Asher

THE LORD RAISED UP JUDGES

and Naphtali in taking over their land comes out tellingly in the comment that they "lived among the Canaanites" (vv. 32, 33).

■ **Judges 2:1-3.** An angelic messenger has not appeared since Joshua's encounter with God's heavenly commander (Joshua 5:13–6:5). The appearance to Joshua brought a positive promise about the coming conquest of the Promised Land. Now the angel declares God's negative judgment against Israel.

■ **Judges 2:6-10.** These verses basically repeat the account of Joshua's death found in Joshua 24:29-31.

■ **Judges 2:11-13.** Canaanite religion centered on the promotion of human, animal, and plant fertility. The ancient inhabitants of the Promised Land saw the focus of divine activity in the formation of new life. As a result of this view, the Canaanites give sexual characteristics to their gods. Baal, whose name means "lord," is the major male deity at this time in Canaan's history. He is thought to appear most clearly in thunderstorms.

The word *Ashtoreth* is the plural form of Asherah. She is Baal's female counterpart. She most clearly manifests as mother earth. In the rain falling from the clouds to earth, the Canaanites see the sexual union of Baal and Asherah as bringing forth all forms of life. Canaanites believe sexual intercourse is a divine activity in which humans may participate. Thus their worship often takes the form of heterosexual intercourse with specially designated priestesses or priests. The Canaanites believe sexual intercourse is a sacred act—the epitome of divinity—not to be abused. Israel's religion, on the other hand, views sex as a gift from God, not an aspect of God's nature.

■ **Judges 2:17.** The image of harlotry is used in the Bible to describe Israel's worship of the Canaanite gods (see Hosea 1:2; 2:1-13). Considering the nature of Canaanite worship, this appears to be an appropriate description.

■ **Judges 2:18.** God acts to save Israel out of pity for the people in their oppression, not because of anything it does.

Although Israel groans and cries out to God (see 3:9), nowhere do we read that the people repent and seek again to serve God.

■ **Judges 2:22–3:2.** God leaves the nations in Israel's midst to test the people's obedience and to teach them war.

■ **Judges 3:7-11.** The cycle repeats of (1) Israel's evil doing, (2) God's punishment, (3) Israel's cry to God, and (4) God's deliverance; but now we learn specifically who is involved. *Cushan-Rishathaim* means "Cushan of double-wickedness." The last part of the name describes the Israelite attitude toward this alien king.

Othniel, the first judge, appeared earlier in Joshua 15:16-19 and its parallel in Judges 1:11-15. As a Kenizzite, Othniel was probably not a member of the community of Israel (see lesson 5). The first deliverer in the Book of Judges is a non-Israelite!

■ **Judges 3:12-13.** Eglon's name means "fat calf" (see v. 17). Moab is the country east of the Promised Land across the Dead Sea. Ammon lies just north of Moab. The Amalekites, a nomadic tribe to the south, often fight against Israel.

■ **Judges 3:15.** Ehud's name possibly means "loner." Being left-handed sets him apart from most people, although this condition may have been common in his tribe (see Judges 20:16). In Israel, as in many cultures, the left side is associated with evil.

■ **Judges 3:16.** Most people, being right-handed, would strap their swords to the left side. Guards looking for hidden weapons would check persons' left sides. By girding his sword on the right, Ehud's weapon escapes detection.

■ **Judges 3:20-23.** Eglon sits in a room on the roof of his house that is covered over for shade but open, or with latticed windows on the sides, so any available breeze can enter. When Ehud announces he has a word from God, Eglon stands up out of respect, making him even more vulnerable to Ehud's attack. God's word for Eglon is the judgment of death.

THE LORD RAISED UP JUDGES

- **Judges 3:27-29.** After blowing a trumpet to summon Israel to holy war, the Israelites seize control of the river crossings and kill off the enemy occupation force as it tries to escape back to Moab.
- **Judges 3:31.** Shamgar's name virtually shouts his non-Israelite status. The name *Shamgar* is probably Hurrian, meaning "Shimike (a god) gave." "Son of Anath" points to his worship of the Canaanite goddess Anath. Not only a non-Israelite, but one who does not worship the Lord, becomes a deliverer of Israel. Shamgar is mentioned again in Judges 5:6.

DIMENSION THREE: WHAT DOES THE BIBLE MEAN TO ME?

Judges 2:6-10—Each Generation Must Know the Lord

Upon the death of Joshua and his generation, no one remains who knows firsthand what God has done for Israel. What happened in the past to Israel no longer speaks directly to the generation now living. These persons must come to know God on their own. When have you tried to pass on to other people things you have learned from past experience?

When have you tried to warn friends or children about something they were facing only to have them ignore your warnings and learn the hard way? Why do people so often appear unable to benefit from the experiences of others? Does this difficulty of learning from the past apply to good experiences as well as bad ones?

How can we learn from others what is most important in our lives? Can we, for example, become close friends with another person by hearing about him or her from a third party? How much would we know about God if we depended on what we heard from others? What can we pass on about God from our experience that may help others come to know God? What can we not pass on? What must each person experience about God directly for himself or herself?

Judges 2:11-18—God's Grace, Not Human Acts

Israel does much to deserve God's punishment, but nothing to merit mercy. Israel groans in oppression, but in the people's cries to God we find no repentance or turning back to the way of the Lord. God delivers the people on the basis of pity for them, not on the basis of any good works they have done.

Do we earn God's deliverance, or does it come in spite of what we do? At what times have you experienced God's grace in your life while at the same time feeling unworthy to receive it? What is the nature of God's love in your life? What does it mean to say God pities us and delivers us before we are faithful to God?

Judges 3:15-23—The Double-edged Sword of Judgment

The Lord raises up a deliverer who takes a message from God to Israel's oppressor. This word takes the form of a double-edged sword that cuts the life from the one who receives it. God's word of judgment remains with its victim; it is not withdrawn.

How do you react to this story? Why? When, if ever, have you seen God's word as a harsh, devastating word of judgment? When have you experienced what you considered to be God's judgment in your life? What happened? Can we reconcile a God who loves and delivers us with a God who also punishes and judges us? How do God's grace and judgment and God's wrath and mercy fit together?

"During Gideon's lifetime, the land enjoyed peace forty years."
(8:28)

9

DEBORAH AND GIDEON

Judges 4–8

DIMENSION ONE: WHAT DOES THE BIBLE SAY?

Answer these questions by reading Judges 4

1. Who leads Israel after Ehud's death? (Judges 4:4)

2. How does Barak respond to the Lord's command given through the prophetess? (Judges 4:8)

3. What does Sisera do when he hears the tribal armies of Zebulun and Naphtali have formed? (Judges 4:12-13)

4. What is the outcome of the battle? (Judges 4:15-17)

5. Why does Sisera flee to the tent of Jael? (Judges 4:17)

6. What does Jael do to Sisera? (Judges 4:21)

GENESIS to REVELATION **JUDGES**

Answer these questions by reading Judges 5

7. Who composes the song found in chapter 5? (Judges 5:1)

8. Which tribes participate in the battle? (Judges 5:14-15, 18)

9. Which tribes are condemned for not taking part in the battle? (Judges 5:15-17)

10. What happens during the battle at Taanach by the waters of Megiddo? (Judges 5:19-21)

Answer these questions by reading Judges 6

11. Where does the angel of the Lord appear to Gideon? (Judges 6:11)

12. What does Gideon say in response to the angel's command to save Israel from the hand of Midian? (Judges 6:15)

13. Why does Gideon go at night to replace Baal's altar and the Asherah pole with an altar to God? (Judges 6:27)

14. Why does Gideon gain the new name Jerub-Baal, "Let Baal contend"? (Judges 6:32)

15. What signs does Gideon demand from God to show that God will indeed save Israel? (Judges 6:36-40)

DEBORAH AND GIDEON

Answer these questions by reading Judges 7

16. Why does God want Gideon's army to be smaller? (Judges 7:2)

17. How does God tell Gideon to reduce his force to only three hundred men? (Judges 7:3-7)

18. What does Gideon overhear when he goes down to the Midianite camp? (Judges 7:13-14)

19. What do Gideon's men do at the outskirts of the Midianite camp? (Judges 7:19-21)

20. What does the Lord do to the Midianites? (Judges 7:22)

Answer these questions by reading Judges 8

21. How do the men of Succoth and Peniel respond to Gideon's request for food? (Judges 8:6, 8)

22. After Gideon captures those he was pursuing, what does he do to Succoth and Peniel? (Judges 8:16-17)

23. Who did Zebah and Zalmunna kill? (Judges 8:19)

24. Why does Gideon reject the offer of the men of Israel to rule over them? (Judges 8:23)

GENESIS to REVELATION **JUDGES**

25. What does Gideon make with the golden earrings his men took as plunder? (Judges 8:24-27)

26. What name does Jerub-Baal give to his son by his concubine in Shechem? (Judges 8:31)

DIMENSION TWO: WHAT DOES THE BIBLE MEAN?

■ **Judges 4:2.** Jabin, king of Hazor, appears also as Joshua's opponent at the Waters of Merom (see Joshua 11).

■ **Judges 4:4.** *Deborah* means "honey bee." She is one of three prophetesses in the Old Testament. The others are Miriam (Exodus 15:20) and Huldah (2 Kings 22:14). Deborah does not share with anyone else her unique status as the only female judge.

■ **Judges 4:5.** Since Deborah judges from within the boundaries of Ephraim, she probably comes from that tribe.

■ **Judges 4:11.** The Kenites claim descent from Cain, the first murderer (see Genesis 4:8-16). Apparently, the Kenites wander through the land as metal workers, or tinkers, selling their services.

■ **Judges 4:16.** No city by this name is known. The name means "wooded hills of the nations" and perhaps refers to a region rather than a city.

■ **Judges 4:21.** Among nomads, the women bear the responsibility for both setting up the tents and striking camp. They often have to drive tent pegs into rocky ground. Jael no doubt has both the skill and strength necessary to drive the peg through Sisera's head.

■ **Judges 5:1.** Since Deborah's name precedes Barak's, she receives primary credit as the composer of the poem, which is known as "The Song of Deborah." This poem, one of the oldest poetic works in the Bible, uses an ancient form of Hebrew that is very difficult to translate.

DEBORAH AND GIDEON

- **Judges 5:4-5.** Mount Seir lies to the southeast of the Dead Sea within the area of Edom.
- **Judges 5:13.** The Israelite force is referred to as "remnant of the nobles" because not all of Israel participates in the battle.
- **Judges 5:19.** Apparently the coalition of Canaanite kings join forces at Taanach on the southern edge of the Plain of Esdraelon. They then journey north and east to meet the Israelites in battle.
- **Judges 5:20-21.** In the uneven confrontation of Canaanite chariots with Israelite infantry, a sudden rainstorm decides the issue. The Kishon River, which drains the plain, overflows. The flood waters sweep the chariots away or bog them down in the mud (compare Exodus 14:25).
- **Judges 5:26-27.** The constant repetition of words describing Sisera's death serves to emphasize the act; much like slow-motion photography depicting violent acts in modern movies.
- **Judges 6:1.** Normally, the Bible portrays Midian as Israel's ally. Moses finds safety in Midian and marries a Midianite wife (Exodus 2:15, 21).
- **Judges 6:5.** The domestication of camels during this period allows the nomads to raid the settled land for supplies and then disappear into the desert.
- **Judges 6:11.** We do not know where to locate Ophrah within Manasseh's territory. Normally, threshing floors were on hilltops so that the breeze could easily carry away the chaff during winnowing. To avoid detection, however, Gideon threshes in a wine press, which was usually a hole sunk in rock where grapes were pressed and their juice collected. Gideon's name means "hewer" or "hacker."
- **Judges 6:27.** This verse clearly reveals a major aspect of Gideon's character: "he was afraid." The theme of fear was hinted at in verse 15 and will continue to reappear throughout the story of Gideon (see 7:3, 10; 8:20).
- **Judges 6:30.** Here Israelites, who should worship only the Lord, want to kill Gideon for doing what God has long commanded (see Exodus 34:12-14; Judges 2:2).

GENESIS to REVELATION **JUDGES**

■ **Judges 6:31-32.** Normally, the name Jerub-Baal would be considered a positive affirmation of faith in Baal's power. Here, Joash uses the name as a challenge to Baal to show how great he is, if he can.

■ **Judges 6:36-40.** Fleece could soak up the dew and remain wet even after the ground had dried in the early morning, but for the fleece to remain dry while the ground around it is covered with dew is unnatural.

■ **Judges 7:3-4.** Sending home the men who are afraid follows the rule for war in Deuteronomy 20:8. Ironically, Gideon, the one who continues as God's chosen, is also afraid (see 7:9-11).

■ **Judges 7:5-6.** No one seems to know what the two modes of drinking reveal about Gideon's men. Perhaps it is an arbitrary way to divide them.

■ **Judges 7:13.** The barley cake symbolizes the settled farmer for whom barley is a major crop. The tent represents the nomad's unsettled life.

■ **Judges 7:19-22.** Gideon's force makes its presence dramatically known. But in a manner typical of a holy war, the Lord accomplishes the victory.

■ **Judges 8:1.** The men of Ephraim, Manasseh's brother tribe, complain because Gideon did not call upon them for help.

■ **Judges 8:2.** Gideon coins a proverb that points out that God has given Ephraim's mop-up operation greater results than Gideon achieved in the initial battle.

■ **Judges 8:4.** Here a new twist to Gideon's story begins, but we do not see it clearly until verses 18-19. Gideon now takes the army called forth by God and uses it to carry out his personal revenge against the Midianite leaders.

■ **Judges 8:5-9.** Succoth and Peniel lie east of Shechem across the Jordan. Both cities reject Gideon's use of Israel's militia for his own purposes.

■ **Judges 8:18-19.** The theme of kingship, which takes up the rest of this chapter and the next (see lesson 10), appears here for the first time.

DEBORAH AND GIDEON

- **Judges 8:20.** Jether, Gideon's eldest son, shares his father's trait of being afraid.
- **Judges 8:21.** Zebah, whose name means "sacrificial victim," and Zalmunna ("protection refused") basically dare Gideon to live up to his name and personally hack them to death.
- **Judges 8:27.** After proclaiming that only the Lord rules in Israel, Gideon makes an ephod that turns Israel away from the proper worship of God. The Bible uses the word *ephod* to refer both to a type of priestly garment and to an object of worship.
- **Judges 8:31.** Although he rejects rule over Israel, Jerub-Baal names one of his sons Abimelek, which means "my father is king"!

DIMENSION THREE: WHAT DOES THE BIBLE MEAN TO ME?

Judges 4:4-9—A Woman's Leadership in Peace and War

Deborah, as prophetess, preaches the word of God. She also serves her people as the presiding officer over all administrative and legal decisions of the Israelite confederacy. Even in time of war, she makes the military decisions and goes onto the battlefield with the army.

How do you react to this biblical portrait of Deborah's role in Israelite affairs? How does this portrait mesh with our own contemporary attitudes about the abilities of women to lead? This biblical understanding indicates that women may be called by God to preach. How does this account address contemporary issues of female participation in religious and political leadership and military action? In what ways might Deborah act as a role model for today's Christian woman?

Judges 6:25-32—Afraid to Contend for the Lord

God commands Gideon to destroy the Canaanite cultic objects and to erect an altar to the Lord. Gideon fulfills God's orders, but he works under the cover of darkness because he is afraid.

Are you ever nervous about expressing your faith openly? When have you held back from saying or doing something you thought was right because you were afraid of ridicule or retaliation? Why do Christians sometimes camouflage their beliefs? Should we always speak and act openly? When is it best to work behind the scenes to do God's will?

Judges 8:4-21—Using God for Our Purposes

Gideon goes beyond God's initial command to deliver Israel from the hand of Midian (6:14). He now uses the power God has given him for his own ends. Gideon uses the army called by God not only to avenge his brothers' deaths but also to punish fellow Israelites who do not agree with what he is doing.

When do we try to use God to achieve our own goals? How can people pervert God's gifts so that they no longer are used for what God intends? Can you think of any persons or groups you perceive to be using religion to achieve nonreligious goals? Why might people do such things? How can we tell when someone is misusing religious belief? In determining our own actions, how can we avoid confusing our desires with God's will?

"Abimelek had governed Israel three years." (9:22)

10

ABIMELEK AND JEPHTHAH

Judges 9–12

DIMENSION ONE: WHAT DOES THE BIBLE SAY?

Answer these questions by reading Judges 9

1. How does Abimelek appeal for the leadership of Shechem? (Judges 9:2)

2. How does Abimelek use the money given him by the men of Shechem? (Judges 9:4)

3. What happens to Abimelek's brothers? (Judges 9:5)

4. What do the citizens of Shechem and Beth Millo do to Abimelek? (Judges 9:6)

5. Who are the main characters in the story that Jotham tells from Mount Gerizim? (Judges 9:8-15)

GENESIS to REVELATION **JUDGES**

6. What curse does Jotham level against Shechem, Beth Millo, and Abimelek? (Judges 9:20)

7. How does God intervene in the relationship between Abimelek and Shechem? (Judges 9:23)

8. How does Abimelek react to the treachery of Shechem? (Judges 9:43-45)

9. How does Abimelek destroy the tower of Shechem? (Judges 9:48-49)

10. What happens to Abimelek when he leads an attack against the tower of Thebez? (Judges 9:52-53)

11. What does Abimelek ask his armor-bearer to do? (Judges 9:54)

Answer these questions by reading Judges 10

12. Who arose after Abimelek? (Judges 10:1, 3)

13. What do the Israelites say to the Lord? (Judges 10:10)

14. How does the Lord respond to Israel's cry for help? (Judges 10:11-14)

ABIMELEK AND JEPHTHAH

Answer these questions by reading Judges 11

15. Who are Jephthah's parents? (Judges 11:1)

16. What do Jephthah's half-brothers do to him? (Judges 11:2)

17. What do the elders of Gilead promise Jephthah if he goes with them to fight the Ammonites? (Judges 11:8-10)

18. Who does Jephthah declare will decide the issue between Israel and Ammon? (Judges 11:27)

19. What vow does Jephthah make to the Lord? (Judges 11:30-31)

20. Who comes forth from Jephthah's house to meet him? (Judges 11:34)

21. What happens for the next two months? (Judges 11:38)

Answer these questions by reading Judges 12

22. Why do the men of Ephraim threaten to burn Jephthah's house with him in it? (Judges 12:1)

23. How do the Gileadites trick Ephraimites trying to escape across the Jordan? (Judges 12:5-6)

24. Who are the next three judges after Jephthah? (Judges 12:8, 11, 13)

DIMENSION TWO: WHAT DOES THE BIBLE MEAN?

■ **Judges 9:1.** Shechem, where Abimelek is made king, was the scene of the covenant ceremony conducted by Joshua (see Joshua 24). Abimelek acts on his own initiative to become a leader over Israel rather than waiting for a call from the Lord.

■ **Judges 9:4.** Baal-Berith, the name of the Canaanite god in Shechem, means "lord of the covenant." Jephthah (Judges 11:3) and David (1 Samuel 22:1-2) also gather private armies from the outcasts of society.

■ **Judges 9:5-6.** In the Bible, the attempt to exterminate all potential rivals often follows on the heels of revolts (see 2 Kings 10:6-7; 11:1-2). The slaying on one stone suggests a sacrificial quality to Abimelek's act.

■ **Judges 9:8-15.** Jotham tells a fable—an instructive tale using plant or animal characters to make its point. Olives, figs, and (grape) vines are three of the most important crops in Palestine. The anti-kingship theme of the story clearly appears in its picture of the useless thornbush as the only one willing to take the job.

■ **Judges 9:16-20.** Jotham here utters one long curse that will become effective only if the Shechemites have not acted in good faith with Jerub-Baal and his house. The rest of the chapter shows how the curse fulfills itself. A word spoken in blessing or curse carries its own power to enact its content.

■ **Judges 9:23.** God also sends an evil spirit between Saul and David (1 Samuel 18:10; 19:9). The early Israelites believed God to be the source of both good and evil, life and death (see esp. 1 Samuel 2:6-8). Since the Lord alone claims control over the world, this belief follows logically.

ABIMELEK AND JEPHTHAH

- **Judges 9:26.** The name *Gaal son of Ebed* reveals his base character, since it means "loathing son of a slave."
- **Judges 9:31.** Abimelek does not reside in Shechem. As the following story shows, Shechem's location makes it difficult to defend. Arumah (v. 41) appears to be about nine miles southeast of Shechem.
- **Judges 9:45.** Abimelek's reason for sowing the ruins of Shechem with salt is not clear. Later Roman practice would suggest that he does it to render the ground infertile.
- **Judges 9:46.** When the outer walls of the city fall to Abimelek, the leaders of Shechem take refuge in the temple of El-Berith ("God of the covenant"). In the time of the judges, temples often were constructed to double as fortresses if the need should arise.
- **Judges 9:54.** Abimelek wishes to avoid the fate of Sisera who died at the hands of a woman (see Judges 5:24-27). To save his honor, he asks his servant to kill him. By this request, Abimelek becomes one of the few suicides in the Bible (see Judges 16:30; Matthew 27:5).
- **Judges 10:1-5.** We find here short notices about two men who judged Israel. A similar, longer list occurs in Judges 12:7-15. No victories against oppressors appear in these lists; only a name, place of residence, perhaps a note on descendants and property, and a place of burial. Since we know so little about these persons, they are often called the minor judges. Some scholars suggest these men are involved strictly with administrative or judicial matters, and not military affairs.
- **Judges 10:10.** These are the only words of confession uttered by the people of Israel in the whole Book of Judges. However, the following verses show that they repent, not because they regret their unfaithfulness to God, but merely to save their own lives.
- **Judges 11:1.** As the illegitimate son of a prostitute, Jephthah has no legal standing in the Israelite community. According to the law in Deuteronomy 23:2, he cannot even participate in the community's worship of the Lord.

GENESIS to REVELATION: JUDGES

■ **Judges 11:4-11.** The elders of Gilead first offer Jephthah the post of temporary military leader. When Jephthah spurns their first offer, they propose making him permanent head over them, if he defeats the Ammonites.

■ **Judges 11:12-23.** Jephthah first tries to resolve the problems through diplomacy. The Ammonite king responds to Jephthah's first inquiry by claiming that Israel took his land. In response to this charge, Jephthah presents Israel's historical claim to the land. Jephthah argues that Israel took the land from the Amorites, not from the Ammonites or Moabites. Consequently, he argues that Ammon has no claim on the land. Verses 19-21 are almost identical to Numbers 21:21-24.

■ **Judges 11:24.** Jephthah assumes that the god Chemosh (a major Moabite god) exists and has power to give land to worshipers. The early Israelites did not deny the existence of other gods. But according to the Lord's commandments, the Israelites were not to be associated with other deities.

■ **Judges 11:26.** The number of years so far given in the Book of judges adds up to three hundred nineteen.

■ **Judges 11:27.** The title *judge* applied to the Lord describes God as the final arbiter of all disputes (see 1 Samuel 24:15).

■ **Judges 11:30-31.** Jephthah does not believe in chance. The Lord controls all events. By leaving indefinite whom he will sacrifice, Jephthah allows the Lord to choose the gift.

■ **Judges 11:34-35.** A vow made to the Lord cannot be withdrawn (see Numbers 30:2; Deuteronomy 23:21-23). Jephthah voluntarily made an agreement with the Lord. He left to God the choice of the gift. Now that the Lord has fulfilled part of the contract, Jephthah cannot back out of his own obligation, no matter how distasteful it has become.

■ **Judges 11:37.** In ancient Israel, a woman's life reached completeness in her marriage and her children (see Genesis 24:60; 30:1). Jephthah's daughter mourns because she will never experience this fulfillment of life.

■ **Judges 11:39.** Israelite religion rejects child sacrifice (see Leviticus 20:1-5). Although God demands that all firstborn creatures be sacrificed (Exodus 22:29-30), children could be redeemed (Exodus 34:20).

The Israelites believed that God sometimes demanded from a person that which he or she most valued. However, they also believed that a person should be willing to give even his or her beloved child to the Lord, if God demanded it (see Genesis 22:1-14). Jephthah offers to give God his best, and the Lord accepts his only child.

■ **Judges 12:1.** The Ephraimites are angry because Jephthah did not enlist their aid in a battle with the Ammonites. Compare Ephraim's similar reaction to Gideon's exploits (Judges 8:1-3).

■ **Judges 12:4.** The deterioration of Israel's covenant community as a result of its broken relationship to God continues. Intertribal warfare breaks out.

■ **Judges 12:6.** The Gileadites base their trick on the fact that the Ephraimites speak a different dialect of Hebrew. The Gileadites force all who want to cross the Jordan to pronounce a *sh* sound. Since the Ephraimites apparently did not use this sound in their speech, men from this tribe could easily be discovered.

■ **Judges 12:8.** This verse tells us that Ibzan followed Jephthah as Israel's judge. Ibzan probably comes from the Bethlehem in Zebulun, not the one in Judah.

DIMENSION THREE: WHAT DOES THE BIBLE MEAN TO ME?

Judges 9:7-15—Can Thorns Give Shade?

Jotham's fable bitterly suggests that people who seek political leadership do not deserve it. He mocks the possibility that those who want to lead can fulfill the promises they so easily make.

What is your opinion about those who seek political office? Do you agree or disagree with Jotham's characterizations? Why? Should religious people become involved in politics? What is the relationship between our religious and political beliefs? How can we discern our Christian responsibility in the political process? How can we implement our faith in our political decisions?

Judges 10:10-16—Self-serving Repentance

Israel calls upon the Lord only when the people need God's help. When God delivers the people, they turn away and ignore God. The people repent now only because they think repentance will get God to do what they want. However, the Lord rejects those who are loyal for selfish purposes.

When do we turn to the Lord? When have you ignored God during good times, only to call upon God when you need help? Why do we worship God? Why do we go to church? Do we serve the Lord out of love or out of self-interest? How can we love God selflessly instead of selfishly? Can we love God for what God is, rather than for what God can do for us?

Judges 11:30-39—What the Lord Requires

Jephthah leaves to the Lord the choice of what will be required to fulfill the vow. Upon Jephthah's return from battle, his daughter comes out to greet him. Jephthah cannot go back on his vow. God requires from him his only child. Jephthah gives her into God's presence.

What does God require from us? What do you value most? Why might God ask you for your most valued possessions? How can such a sacrifice express our love for God? In this context, what does it mean that God sacrificed Jesus for us? Does God ask any more from us than we have already been given? If so, what?

"Having put him to sleep on her lap, she called a man to shave off the seven braids of his hair, and so began to subdue him."
(16:19)

11
SAMSON THE NAZIRITE
Judges 13–16

DIMENSION ONE: WHAT DOES THE BIBLE SAY?

Answer these questions by reading Judges 13

1. What does the angel of the Lord say to the wife of Manoah? (Judges 13:3)

2. What must never happen to the woman's child? (Judges 13:5)

3. What limitations does the angel place upon the woman? (Judges 13:13-14)

4. What does the angel say when Manoah asks his name? (Judges 13:18)

5. What happens when Manoah makes his offering? (Judges 13:20)

6. Why does Manoah's wife conclude they will not die? (Judges 13:23)

Answer these questions by reading Judges 14

7. What does Samson demand from his parents after his trip to Timnah? (Judges 14:2)

8. Why is Samson attracted to the Philistine woman? (Judges 14:4)

9. What happens in the vineyards of Timnah? (Judges 14:5-6)

10. What does Samson find when he turns aside on a later journey to Timnah? (Judges 14:8)

11. How do the Philistines extort the answer to Samson's riddle from his wife? (Judges 14:15)

12. How does Samson pay off his debt to the thirty men? (Judges 14:19)

SAMSON THE NAZIRITE

Answer these questions by reading Judges 15

13. What does Samson do to the Philistine fields when he finds his wife has been given to another man? (Judges 15:4-5)

14. How do the Philistines avenge what Samson has done to their fields? (Judges 15:6)

15. Why do the three thousand men of Judah come to Samson's place of refuge at the rock of Etam? (Judges 15:12)

16. What happens when the men of Judah deliver Samson to the Philistines? (Judges 15:14-15)

Answer these questions by reading Judges 16

17. What does Samson do to the gates of Gaza? (Judges 16:3)

18. With whom does Samson fall in love? (Judges 16:4)

19. What do the rulers of the Philistines offer Samson's beloved to deliver him into their power? (Judges 16:5)

20. How does Delilah strip Samson of his strength? (Judges 16:19)

21. How do the Philistines treat Samson once they capture him? (Judges 16:21)

22. Why do the Philistines call Samson into the house of their god Dagon? (Judges 16:25)

23. How does Samson kill himself and all the people in the house? (Judges 16:29-30)

DIMENSION TWO: WHAT DOES THE BIBLE MEAN?

■ **Judges 13:1.** With the Samson accounts, the Philistines appear as an active oppressor of Israel. From now until the time of David, the Philistines are the major threat to Israel's existence.
■ **Judges 13:2.** The city of Zorah lies fourteen miles west of Jerusalem. Manoah's name means "rest."
■ **Judges 13:3.** The theme of the barren wife to whom God grants a child is popular in the Bible (see the story of Sarah beginning in Genesis 16:1, and the birth of Samuel in 1 Samuel 1:1-20).
■ **Judges 13:4-7.** Numbers 6:1-21 contains the laws concerning Nazirites. Normally, the vow for a Nazirite is temporary. During the designated period, the Nazirite has to maintain ritual purity. Also, Nazirites can neither drink alcoholic beverages nor cut their hair. Manoah's wife adds to the angel's words that her son will be a Nazirite "until the day of his death."
■ **Judges 13:17.** Manoah's request for a name shares the same desire to know and control the divine that we find in the story of Moses at the burning bush (see Exodus 3:13-15).

- **Judges 13:22.** Israel believed that no mortal could bear to look upon God and live (see also Exodus 33:20).
- **Judges 13:24.** Samson's name means either "little sun" or "solar one." "Sunny" would be a good translation.
- **Judges 14:1.** Timnah lies six miles west of Zorah. This proximity shows how closely Samson's tribe of Dan lives to the Philistines. Pressure from the Philistines will soon force the tribe of Dan to leave its original territory and search for new land (see lesson 12).
- **Judges 14:2-3.** Samson's parents are reluctant to let him marry a Philistine woman. The Israelites were not supposed to intermarry with the inhabitants of the land (see Joshua 23:12-13).
- **Judges 14:5.** The Asian lion of this period was smaller than the African lion we normally see.
- **Judges 14:8-10.** We begin to discover that Samson does not take his Nazirite vow very seriously. The Nazirite is forbidden to go near any kind of corpse (see Numbers 6:6). In verse 10, the word *feast* literally means a drinking session. Again, we see that Samson does not faithfully follow his calling.
- **Judges 14:14.** By nature, a riddle tries to deceive its listener into giving the wrong answer. In the wedding feast setting, the most natural answers to this riddle would be either *vomit* (see Proverbs 26:11) or *sexual intercourse* (see Proverbs 30:20).
- **Judges 14:18.** The Philistines couch their answer in the form of a mocking riddle whose answer should be *love*. Samson clearly sees the source for their answer. A *heifer* was a common ancient metaphor for wife.
- **Judges 14:19.** Ashkelon, one of the major cities of the Philistines, lies on the coast northwest of Timnah. Samson gets the last laugh. Since the Philistines did not win the riddle contest fairly, Samson does not pay off his debt fairly. He kills thirty Philistines of Ashkelon to clothe thirty Philistines in Timnah.

- **Judges 15:1.** Samson apparently enters in to a marriage where his wife stays with her family and he visits her there.
- **Judges 15:4-5.** Samson's attack on the fields during harvest (see v. 1) is especially devastating. Loss of food for the next year could result in starvation.
- **Judges 15:6-8.** Samson's wife places her loyalty to her father and people over her loyalty to her husband. However, the Philistines see her only as a means to avenge themselves on Samson. Samson now enters into a blood vengeance feud with the Philistines.
- **Judges 15:11.** To the men of Judah, Samson claims that he has done nothing more than fulfill the law of retribution: "You are to take life for life, eye for eye, tooth for tooth" (Exodus 21:23-24).
- **Judges 15:12-13.** The breakdown of intertribal unity is clearly evident in these verses. The men of Judah willingly betray a fellow Israelite into the hands of the Philistines.
- **Judges 15:15.** A fresh jawbone would be hard and resilient, easily used as an effective club. However, an old jawbone would be too dry and brittle to be used as a weapon.
- **Judges 15:20.** Normally this type of summary statement concludes an account of the total activity of a judge (see, e.g., Judges 12:7). However, we still have more to learn about Samson.
- **Judges 16:1-3.** Gaza, the southernmost of the five major Philistine cities, is located about a mile from the Mediterranean Sea.

City gates had to be massive in order to withstand military assault. By taking Gaza's gates, Samson opens the city to attack. Hebron, the place to which Samson carries the gates, lies forty miles east of Gaza.

- **Judges 16:4-5.** In these verses, Delilah is introduced for the first time. She comes from the region of "the Valley of Sorek." Zorah and Timnah, the scenes of Samson's earliest adventures, are also in the Valley of Sorek.

Although Delilah is commonly called a Philistine, she was probably an Israelite. This would explain why the Philistine lords have to bribe her.

- **Judges 16:11.** New ropes would, by nature, be stronger than older ones. Their newness also lends a certain magical quality to their power.
- **Judges 16:13-14.** Weaving a person's hair into the taut threads of a loom would tie him or her down quite effectively. However, Samson rips the loom apart when he jumps up.
- **Judges 16:17-20.** This is the only time Samson mentions his status as a Nazirite. Samson has often broken his Nazirite vow, but his confession to Delilah is the final betrayal of that vow. With the cutting of his hair, the Nazirite vow ends. Samson's special sanctity and power also cease.
- **Judges 16:21.** The Philistines seize Samson and gouge out his eyes. Blinding a captured enemy was not uncommon in the ancient world. King Zedekiah was blinded by the Babylonians after he was captured (see 2 Kings 25:7). The Philistines then force Samson to turn the mill, a task usually done by a blindfolded beast of burden.
- **Judges 16:23.** Dagon is the Canaanite god of grain. Apparently the Philistines took over the worship of Dagon when they entered Palestine shortly after the Israelites.
- **Judges 16:28.** In his request to God, Samson asks to go beyond the rule of an eye for an eye. He wants to kill all the Philistines in the house of Dagon.
- **Judges 16:31.** Like Jephthah, Samson has no children to survive him. The responsibility for his burial, which normally would be his children's, falls instead on Samson's brothers.

DIMENSION THREE: WHAT DOES THE BIBLE MEAN TO ME?

Judges 13: 15-20—Desire to Detain the Holy

Manoah asks the angel of the Lord to remain a while. He does not want to release the person who has brought this happy message from God. Manoah wants to know all he can about this visitor from God. However, in the end, the white heat of this divine encounter disappears with the flame into heaven. Manoah is left lying on the ground.

When have you experienced joyous or exciting occasions that you did not want to end? Why do we want to hold on to such moments? Do we feel let down when such times come to an end? Why?

Can we possess the ecstatic moments in our lives? Should we try? How do these moments of special intimacy, joy, or excitement fit into the totality of our lives? How does personal religious experience enter into this discussion? What is it like to experience God as especially close? Are such experiences characteristic of your faith? How do you experience God?

Judges 15:14-20—Putting Our Deeds in Perspective

The Spirit of the Lord makes it possible for Samson to slay a thousand of his enemies. In his song celebrating the event, Samson sings as if he did it all alone, without God's help. But his thirst quickly reminds him of his own mortality. He finds that he cannot really save himself. He must call upon God for deliverance.

Do you usually take the credit for your successes? Do you also take responsibility for your failures? In the successes and failures of our lives, how much responsibility comes from us and how much comes from God?

SAMSON THE NAZIRITE

Judges 16:28-31—Vengeance Destroys the Avenger

Much of Samson's life is taken up with seeking vengeance against those he believes have wronged him. Here the cycle of vengeance has grown to the point that Samson kills more than three thousand people to avenge "my two eyes." The final tragedy is that Samson wills his own death in order to get his revenge.

When have you tried to get even with those who hurt or insulted you? How do you feel when you retaliate against someone? How do you feel when you are the victim of someone's revenge? Does the search for retaliation make a bad situation better or worse? Where does the desire for vengeance eventually lead? How can we avoid being vengeful? Why should we as Christians try not to be vindictive?

GENESIS to REVELATION **JUDGES**

"In those days Israel had no king." (18:1)

12

MICAH AND THE DANITES
Judges 17–21

DIMENSION ONE: WHAT DOES THE BIBLE SAY?

Answer these questions by reading Judges 17

1. How much money had Micah stolen from his mother? (Judges 17:2)

2. What does Micah's mother do with the returned money? (Judges 17:4)

3. What is the political situation in Israel at this time? (Judges 17:6)

4. What does Micah offer the young Levite? (Judges 17:10)

Answer these questions by reading Judges 18

5. Why do the Danites send five men to spy out the land? (Judges 18:1-2)

MICAH AND THE DANITES

6. How does the priest respond to the Danites' question about their journey? (Judges 18:6)

7. What kind of people do the five spies find in Laish? (Judges 18:7)

8. When the Danites return to Micah's house, what do they do? (Judges 18:17-18)

9. How do the Danites convince the priest to go with them? (Judges 18:19)

10. What do the Danites do to the city of Laish? (Judges 18:27)

Answer these questions by reading Judges 19

11. Why does the Levite from Ephraim go to Bethlehem in Judah? (Judges 19:2-3)

12. Why does the Levite refuse to turn aside at Jebus on his return home? (Judges 19:11-12)

13. Who finally offers the Levite a place to stay in Gibeah? (Judges 19:16, 20)

14. What do the wicked men of Gibeah demand concerning the visitor? (Judges 19:22)

GENESIS to REVELATION JUDGES

15. Who does the Levite's host offer to give to the men? (Judges 19:24)

16. What does the Levite find in the morning when he opens the door of the house? (Judges 19:27)

17. Upon arriving home, what does the Levite do to his concubine? (Judges 19:29)

Answer these questions by reading Judges 20

18. What accusation does the Levite make against the men of Gibeah in Benjamin? (Judges 20:5)

19. How does the tribe of Benjamin respond to Israel's demand to turn over the offenders for execution? (Judges 20:13-14)

20. How many Israelites fall before the Benjamite army in the first two battles? (Judges 20:21, 25)

21. How does Israel finally defeat Benjamin? (Judges 20:36-37, 40-43)

22. How many Benjamite males survive the battle? (Judges 20:47)

MICAH AND THE DANITES

Answer these questions by reading Judges 21

23. What had the men of Israel sworn at Mizpah? (Judges 21:1)

24. Why do the people weep at Bethel? (Judges 21:2-3)

25. Why does Israel slaughter everyone but the virgins in Jabesh Gilead? (Judges 21:8-14)

26. What do the elders of the congregation tell the Benjamites to do in order to get the wives they need? (Judges 21:20-21)

27. How does this plan by the elders keep Israel from violating its oath? (Judges 21:22)

DIMENSION TWO: WHAT DOES THE BIBLE MEAN?

■ **Judges 17:1.** Micah's name is an exclamatory question meaning "Who is comparable to Yahweh?"

■ **Judges 17:2-4.** In an attempt to avoid destruction from his mother's curse, Micah returns the stolen money. His mother now speaks a word of blessing to try to cancel the curse. Micah's mother consecrates the returned money to God's service.

However, by having an image of the Lord constructed she breaks one of the major commandments: "You shall not make for yourself an image" (Exodus 20:4). Verse 3 is not talking about two separate images. The carved image is a wooden object that is covered with the silver cast image.

GENESIS to REVELATION **JUDGES**

■ **Judges 17:5.** Micah fills his shrine with the proper furnishings. For information about the ephod, see lesson 9, on Judges 8:27. The idols are Micah's personal family gods. In the popular belief of the day, these family gods watch out for the family's benefit in the heavenly court. This chapter clearly shows how much Israel's view of the Lord has come under the influence of other religions.

■ **Judges 17:6.** This statement serves almost as a refrain throughout the last five chapters of Judges (see Judges 18:1; 19:1; 21:25). The phrase indicates that there is no longer any centralized order in Israel. Anarchy reigns.

■ **Judges 17:7.** *Levite* appears here as a class or profession rather than as a tribe. This Levite belongs to the tribe of Judah. Since the Levites have no inheritance in the land, their official status is that of sojourners, or resident aliens. Deuteronomy 14:28-29 classes them, along with orphans and widows, as persons needing charity.

■ **Judges 18:1.** For other accounts of Dan's original territory and why this tribe was forced to migrate, see Joshua 19:40-48; Judges 1:34. From the preceding stories concerning Samson, it appears that Philistine pressure causes the Danites to seek new land.

■ **Judges 18:2.** Zorah was Samson's hometown (see Judges 13:2). Eshtaol is only a few miles northeast of Zorah.

■ **Judges 18:3.** The Danites probably recognize the Levite's southern accent, since it was similar to their own. The town of Bethlehem is about fifteen miles east of Zorah and Eshtaol.

■ **Judges 18:7.** In Joshua 19:47, Laish is called Leshem. This town lies along the far northern border of the Promised Land, north of the Sea of Galilee. Sidon is a Phoenician city on the Mediterranean coast.

■ **Judges 18:10.** The Danites win over the priest by pointing out the advantage of a larger parish.

■ **Judges 18:24-26.** Since the Danites have already been squeezed out of their territory, they are desperate people, who have little to lose. Micah discovers that the curse his

MICAH AND THE DANITES

mother unknowingly put upon him was not completely canceled by her blessing and the Levite's presence. He has nothing but his life.

- **Judges 18:29.** The birth of Dan is reported in Genesis 30:5-6. Dan was the son of Rachel and Jacob (by Rachel's maid, Bilhah).
- **Judges 18:30.** This verse reveals the startling claim that the young Levite, who serves first Micah's shrine and then the tribe of Dan, is a direct descendant of Moses. "The time of the captivity of the land" refers to the destruction of the Northern Kingdom of Israel in 722 BC (see 2 Kings 17:1-6).
- **Judges 19:4-8.** The lavish hospitality shown by the Levite's father-in-law contrasts starkly with the events about to occur in Gibeah. The only hospitality shown in Gibeah is by an aged Ephraimite who resides there (see vv. 15-21).
- **Judges 19:10-13.** Jerusalem is about a mile off the main north-south road and five miles north of Bethlehem. Gibeah, meaning "hill," lies three miles north of Jerusalem. Two miles farther north we find Ramah, meaning "height."
- **Judges 19:22.** The "wicked men" of the town demand that the visitor be brought out to them so that they can have sex with him. Lot's angelic visitors in Sodom faced a similar demand (see Genesis 19:5).
- **Judges 19:23-24.** The rules of hospitality in Israel require that the host protect his or her guests at all costs. The man from Ephraim offers his own daughter and the Levite's concubine for the men to ravish (compare Genesis 19:8). That the female guest does not receive the same protection as the male signals a different level of regard for women.
- **Judges 19:25.** Early in the period of the judges, women could participate fully in the community. This verse reveals how much Israelite belief in the value of women has deteriorated. Rather than being full members of the covenant community, women are now seen merely as objects to be used at the discretion of men. As much as Micah's idols, this attitude shows Israel's distance from the Lord.

- **Judges 19:29.** This verse does not clearly state that the concubine was dead before the Levite divides her into pieces! Considering his callousness the night before, we should not fill in the silence of the text on this matter.
- **Judges 20:13.** When the Israelites demand that the men of Gibeah be given over to them, strong tribal solidarity keeps Benjamin from turning over the guilty persons.
- **Judges 20:16.** Earlier Ehud used his left-handedness to carry out God's will (Judges 3:15-30). These Benjamite slingers use their left-handedness to defend those who have broken God's commandments.
- **Judges 20:28.** Only on this third occasion does the Lord finally promise Israel victory. How or why a vastly outnumbered Benjamin defeats the rest of the tribes is never explained. Israel believes both victory and defeat come from the Lord. Consequently, God must will the defeat of Israel.
- **Judges 20:29-36.** Israel uses the same tactic against the Benjamites in Gibeah as it did under Joshua against Ai (see Joshua 8:3-23).
- **Judges 20:35.** Since Benjamin had mustered twenty-six thousand seven hundred men (see v.15), this verse suggests there should be sixteen hundred survivors. Another tradition lists the total number of casualties as twenty-five thousand "valiant fighters" (v. 46).
- **Judges 21:3.** With the tribe of Benjamin on the verge of destruction, the wholeness of all Israel is threatened. With the Israelite understanding of the community as one body, to lose a part is to risk losing all. The people ask God why this should happen. Unfortunately, they do not await God's answer. They take the initiative to restore Benjamin.
- **Judges 21:8.** Jabesh Gilead lies east of the Jordan, about fourteen miles north of the Jabbok River.
- **Judges 21:8-12.** Refusing to participate in the assembly of tribes at Mizpah is judged a capital offense. The primary motive for the destruction of this city is to find a means to circumvent Israel's oath not to give its daughters in marriage to Benjamin.

MICAH AND THE DANITES

- **Judges 21:13-14.** Since the fathers of the virgins of Jabesh Gilead are dead, the Israelite oath is not broken. They do not give their daughters to Benjamin; they give someone else's daughters. However, there are not enough virgins to fulfill the need for wives for the men of Benjamin.
- **Judges 21:20-22.** The elders of Israel arrange for the Benjamite men to steal the rest of the wives they need during the feast at Shiloh. Again, this arrangement technically keeps Israel from breaking its oath not to give its daughters to Benjamin. The men of Benjamin take the daughters; they are not given to them. Israel circumvents its oath and restores Benjamin, but at the cost of many lives and its integrity.
- **Judges 21:25.** The truth of this concluding statement has been graphically depicted throughout the last five chapters.

DIMENSION THREE: WHAT DOES THE BIBLE MEAN TO ME?

Judges 18:14-20—Why Should Pastors Move?

While the Danites plunder Micah's shrine, they offer his Levite the chance to move from being priest of one house to being priest of a whole tribe. The Levite finds this offer too attractive to reject. He goes with the tribe to its new city in the far north.

Do you consider the offer of a larger, more prestigious church a justifiable reason for a pastor to move? For what valid reasons might a pastor move? For what valid reasons might a pastor change his or her place of service? What are some specific criteria a pastor could use to decide whether to move to a new setting? How can a church know whether it needs to request a different pastor? How can the pairing of church and pastor be done in a Christian way?

Judges 19:10-30—The Visitor in Our Midst

The Levite goes to Gibeah, assuming he will be well received among fellow Israelites. However, no native of the town extends him a welcome. When the Levite does find lodging, the men of the city come to use him for their own purposes. When they cannot have the Levite, they so abuse his concubine that morning finds her silent at the threshold.

Although this Levite's experience of rejection was quite extreme, it still might raise for us the question of how your church welcomed newcomers. When have you been a visitor to a church that did not seem to welcome you? How did you feel as a result? How does your church integrate new members into its midst? What are some specific ways we can make new persons feel that they are part of our church?

Judges 21:16-24—Destroying Our Own

The Israelites have almost totally destroyed the tribe of Benjamin. Almost too late, they realize the wholeness of the twelve tribes is about to end. Although they have made foolish statements that limit their options for reconciliation, the Israelites finally do what is necessary to save Benjamin.

Think about the times when you have been part of a family or church that split apart over some issue. What was the outcome in these situations? Why do some of the worst conflicts take place within families or close-knit groups? Why do we so often attack those closest to us? What causes friends to turn on each other? How can we avoid saying or doing things that will drive off those we love? What can we do to reconcile with persons with whom we have fought?

"Where you go I will go. . . . Your people will be my people and your God my God." (1:16)

13
THE STORY OF RUTH
Ruth 1–4

DIMENSION ONE: WHAT DOES THE BIBLE SAY?

Answer these questions by reading Ruth 1

1. Why does the family of Elimelek move from Judah to Moab? (Ruth 1:1-2)

2. What were the names of Mahlon's and Kilion's wives? (Ruth 1:3-5)

3. How does Naomi respond when her daughters-in-law first refuse to leave her? (Ruth 1:11-13)

4. How does Ruth respond to Naomi's request that she return to her people? (Ruth 1:16-17)

5. What name does Naomi give herself? Why? (Ruth 1:20-21)

6. What important agricultural event is occurring when Ruth and Naomi return to Bethlehem? (Ruth 1:22)

Answer these questions by reading Ruth 2

7. Who is Boaz? (Ruth 2:1)

8. Why does Ruth come to the part of the field belonging to Boaz? (Ruth 2:3)

9. What does Boaz say to Ruth at their first meeting? (Ruth 2:8-9)

10. Why has Ruth found favor in Boaz's eyes? (Ruth 2:11)

11. What recompense for Ruth does Boaz ask from the Lord? (Ruth 2:12)

12. What happens at mealtime? (Ruth 2:14)

13. How does Naomi react when she finds out Ruth has worked in Boaz's field? (Ruth 2:20)

Answer these questions by reading Ruth 3

14. What does Naomi tell Ruth to do on the night Boaz is winnowing barley? (Ruth 3:3-4)

THE STORY OF RUTH

15. What does Ruth tell Boaz to do when he discovers her beside him? (Ruth 3:9)

16. How does Boaz reply to Ruth's request? (Ruth 3:10-11)

17. What problem stands in the way of Boaz fulfilling Ruth's request? (Ruth 3:12-13)

Answer these questions by reading Ruth 4

18. What does Boaz first say to the guardian-redeemer at the city gate? (Ruth 4:3-4)

19. How does the guardian-redeemer react when he finds he must take Ruth when he buys Elimelek's land? (Ruth 4:5-6)

20. After the first guardian-redeemer refuses to redeem the land and Ruth, what does Boaz do? (Ruth 4:9-10)

21. What blessing do the people and elders pronounce after they have witnessed Boaz's statement? (Ruth 4:11-12)

22. What name do the women give to Ruth and Boaz's child? (Ruth 4:17)

23. What important Old Testament person descended from Ruth? (Ruth 4:17)

DIMENSION TWO: WHAT DOES THE BIBLE MEAN?

■ **Ruth 1:1.** Moab lies southeast of Bethlehem across the Dead Sea. Although Moab and Israel shared similar languages and customs, they were often at odds with each other.

■ **Ruth 1:5.** In Israel's male-dominated society, a woman was a person only insofar as she was related to a man. Consequently, a woman who has lost both husband and sons has little hope. She has no one to provide for her.

■ **Ruth 1:11-13.** Naomi's words refer to an Israelite custom, the levirate marriage. When a man died before having a son, his brother or nearest male relative was to marry the dead man's wife. The first male child born to this union then became the legal descendant and heir of the deceased (see Deuteronomy 25:5-10).

■ **Ruth 1:16-17.** Ruth here takes a solemn vow in the name of Naomi's God to stay with her, in both life and death. Oaths in God's name are taken extremely seriously in the Bible (see Exodus 20:7; Judges 11:35-39).

■ **Ruth 1:20.** Naomi reveals her bitterness toward God for what has happened to her. She requests that her name be changed from *Naomi*, which means "pleasant," to *Mara*, which means "bitter." Israel was not afraid to confront God as the cause of all that happened, both good and bad.

■ **Ruth 1:21.** This contrast of *empty* and *full* will be repeated throughout the book.

■ **Ruth 1:22.** This verse marks a turning point in the downward direction of Naomi and Ruth's story. The return to Bethlehem, which means "house of bread" (in itself a name of hope), comes on the joyous occasion of the barley harvest. This is the first harvest of the Palestinian agricultural year. Worries over last year's dwindling food supply can now cease. New food means new hope for a full life. Israel celebrates the Passover during this happy time.

THE STORY OF RUTH

- **Ruth 2:1.** Boaz's character is revealed by his name, which means "strength is in him."
- **Ruth 2:2.** An Israelite farmer does not totally clean his field after he harvests it. The grain that has been missed or accidentally dropped is left for widows, strangers, and orphans to gather or glean.
- **Ruth 2:12.** The "wings" of God were symbols of God's protection of the people (see Psalm 91:4).
- **Ruth 2:20.** *Guardian-redeemer* refers to a specific relative whose special duty is to protect the family's rights. He also redeems, or buys back, land that might pass from the family's ownership.
- **Ruth 3:2.** Winnowing occurs after the grain heads have been broken by flailing or dragging a sledge over them. The grain is thrown into the air. The wind blows away the lighter chaff, but the heavier kernels fall to the threshing floor to be gathered up.
- **Ruth 3:3.** Ruth is to make herself enticing. During harvest festivals, behavior not normally allowed by Israelite society was tolerated in the joyousness of the celebration. Remember, for example, the incident in Judges 21:20-23, where the tribe of Benjamin steals brides at the feast of Shiloh (see lesson 12).
- **Ruth 3:4.** The word translated *feet* refers literally to the lower part of the body. But the Bible also commonly uses the word to refer to sexual organs (see Exodus 4:25; Isaiah 6:2).
- **Ruth 3:9.** The word translated *garment* is the same word as *wings* used in Boaz's blessing in 2:12. Apparently, placing a portion of the man's garment over the woman was part of the marriage ceremony in Israel (see Ezekiel 16:8). Ruth here asks Boaz to consummate marriage with her.
- **Ruth 3:12-13.** Boaz informs Ruth that he is not legally her redeemer. There is a male relative who is more closely related. However, Boaz promises he will marry Ruth if the other man does not.

■ **Ruth 3:14.** Ruth still spends the night with Boaz, lying beside him. Boaz shows concern—either for Ruth's honor or for his plans for the coming day—in his warning that no one should know she is there.

■ **Ruth 4:1-2.** Here we see Israelite legal procedure at work. Judgments are made at the city gate in special areas set aside for such purposes. Since everyone passes through the gate in the morning to go to the fields, persons could easily be called aside to participate in legal matters. The older, more experienced residents of the town are called upon to witness the outcome.

■ **Ruth 4:3-6.** The nearer kinsman, who is never named, accepts his role as redeemer for the land that is about to be sold. More land means more food and a greater inheritance for his children. But he declines when he learns he must also marry Ruth. He would have to support her, her future children, and probably Naomi as well. Then Naomi's land would belong to the firstborn male child, the legal heir of Elimelek, and not to the kinsman. In other words, the kinsman sees at least twenty years of work on the land, three more mouths to feed, and nothing to pass along to his own children out of the deal. This, he decides, he cannot do.

■ **Ruth 4:7-8.** Giving the sandal to the other appears to be close to our own custom of signing our names to a legal transaction. The nearer kinsman "signs" over to Boaz his rights to the land and to Ruth.

■ **Ruth 4:12.** We find a reference here to the only other levirate marriage recorded in the Bible, that of Tamar and Judah in Genesis 38.

■ **Ruth 4:13.** This is the only verse in the book that speaks about God's active involvement in what happens to Ruth. Through God's intervention, Ruth conceives a child by Boaz.

■ **Ruth 4:15.** Israel valued sons more highly than daughters. Seven was the perfect number of sons to have (see Job 1:2). To say Ruth is worth more than seven sons reveals how highly she is honored and respected.

■ **Ruth 4:17.** The story concludes with a final twist. The great-grandson of the non-Israelite Ruth turns out to be the greatest king over all Israel—David.

DIMENSION THREE: WHAT DOES THE BIBLE MEAN TO ME?

Ruth 1:1-21—Questioning God's Faithfulness

We see in this passage the destruction of almost everything that gives meaning to Israel's life. The coming of a famine exiles Elimelek's family from their homeland. They must flee to survive. Although they are strangers in an enemy country, they still have one another. But then the family itself disintegrates. First the father, then the sons, die. All human hopes, dreams, and attachments are shattered. Naomi, feeling alone and bitter, tries to push away the people who still care for her. Ruth refuses to leave, but Naomi still cries out against God.

How do we feel when things we are attached to, or persons we love, are taken from us? Are we willing at these times to admit our bitterness toward God? Why are we afraid to accept our negative feelings about God? Does true faith ever involve doubting or questioning God? Do we trust God's love enough that we can complain to God as Jesus did on the cross, "My God, my God, why have you forsaken me" (Matthew 27:46)?

Ruth 1:22–2:7—God's Providence

Ruth and Naomi return at harvest, the right time in Israel to come home. Ruth "happened" to come to Boaz's field, where he notices her. The Bible normally portrays God working for the people's good, not through dramatic miracles, but through the ordinary occurrences in their lives. Have you ever experienced God working in your life in some ordinary event? If so, which event or events? Why do we concentrate so much of our attention on the dramatic interventions of God? Is God always at work in our lives? Or does God act only at special moments?

Ruth 4:1-22—Restored to Fullness

The fullness in life that was lost in the beginning of the story is now completely restored. The harvest is over and the famine dispelled. Boaz successfully carries out his responsibility to redeem Ruth and Naomi. The family is restored to wholeness by the marriage of Ruth and Boaz and the birth of their son. Naomi's personal life is now full again as she sees her grandchild in her lap. Through all the apparent human emptiness, God has worked to bring fullness. Out of the darkness of human emptiness God brings salvation.

When has your life lost its fullness and meaning? At these times, how did God work to restore that fullness of life? What made you aware of God's restoration?

GLOSSARY OF TERMS

Abimelek: the son of Gideon who was king of Shechem for a brief period (see esp. Judges 9)

Achan: a man from the tribe of Judah whose theft of booty devoted to God resulted in his death (see esp. Joshua 7–8)

Adani-Zedek: the king of Jerusalem, who allied with four other kings against Joshua and his army (Joshua 10:1, 3)

Ai: a Canaanite city captured by Joshua in the conquest (see esp. Joshua 7–8)

Amalekites: a nomadic tribe often involved in conflict with the Israelites (Judges 3:13; 6:3, 33; 7:12; 10:12; 12:15)

Amorites: various Semitic people who settled in Mesopotamia, Syria, and Palestine (see esp. Joshua 10; 13; 24; Judges 11)

Amman: the territory just north of Moab (Judges 11:27)

Anakites: a legendary race of giants living in Canaan (Joshua 11:21-22; 14:12, 15)

Asherah: the female counterpart of Baal (Judges 6:25-30)

Ashkelan: a major Philistine city on the coast of Palestine (Joshua 13:3; Judges 1:18; 14:19)

Baal: the main Canaanite deity at the time of the conquest (see esp. Judges 2; 6)

Ban: a decree that required the absolute destruction of everything within a conquered city (see Joshua 6:18)

Barak: an Israelite who, together with the prophetess Deborah, defeated Sisera (see esp. Judges 4)

Bethel: a Canaanite city founded by Jacob, located near Ai (see esp. Joshua 8; Judges 20–21)

Bethlehem: the city south of Jerusalem where Ruth and Naomi settled (see esp. Ruth 1:1-2, 19, 22)

Beth Millo: a fortress in the middle of the city of Shechem (Judges 9:6, 20)

Bezer: a city of refuge located east of the Jordan (Joshua 20:8; 21:36)

Boaz: the husband of Ruth (Ruth 2–4)

Book of Jashar: a well-known collection of war poetry that circulated in ancient Israel (Joshua 10:13)

Caleb: one of the spies who first entered Canaan; he received the city of Hebron as his inheritance (see esp. Joshua 15)

Canaanites: non-Israelite inhabitants of the Promised Land (see esp. Joshua 17; Judges 1)

Chemosh: a Moabite deity (Judges 11:24)

Dagon: a major Philistine deity (Judges 16:23)

Deborah: an Israelite prophetess who, along with Barak, defeated the army of Sisera (Judges 4–5)

Delilah: an Israelite woman, beloved by Samson (Judges 16)

Eglon: the Moabite king defeated by Ehud (see esp. Judges 3:12-30)

Ehud: an Israelite who defeated the Moabites and brought rest to Israel for two generations (see esp. Judges 3:12-30)

Eleazar: the son of Aaron, heir to the priesthood (see Numbers 3:2; Joshua 14:1; 17:4; 19:51; 22:13; 24:33)

Elimelek: Ruth's father-in-law (Ruth 1:2-3; 2:1, 3; 4:3, 9)

Ephod: a type of priestly garment and an object of worship (see esp. Judges 18:14-17)

Ephmim: territory of the tribe of Ephraim, west of the Jordan River (see esp. Joshua 16; 21; Judges 12)

Gaal: a Canaanite who persuaded the people of Shechem to revolt against their king, Abimelek (Judges 9:26-41)

Gibeah: a city near Jerusalem, later inhabited by Saul (see esp. Judges 20)

Gibeath Haaraloth: a hill near Gilgal where circumcisions were performed (Joshua 5:3)

Gibeon: a city that allied with Joshua against five Amorite cities (see esp. Joshua 10:1-15)

Gideon: from the tribe of Manasseh, one of the judges of Israel (Judges 6–8)

GLOSSARY OF TERMS

Gilead: a term used in different places in the Bible to refer to a tribe, a city, and a territory (see esp. Judges 10–12)

Gilgal: a campsite of the Israelites when they first entered the Promised Land (see esp. Joshua 4:19–5:12; 10:5-13)

Hazor: a city in northern Canaan captured by Joshua and his army (see esp. Joshua 11:10-13; Judges 4:1-2)

Hebron: a city south of Jerusalem, captured by Joshua and his army during the conquest (see esp. Joshua 10:36-43)

Jabesh Gilead: a city whose inhabitants were slaughtered by the Israelites (Judges 21)

Jabin: the king of Hazor who was defeated and killed by Joshua and his army (Joshua 11:1-11; Judges 4)

Jael: the nomadic woman who killed Sisera after he was defeated by the Israelites (Judges 4–5)

Jephthah: an Israelite who delivered the people from the Ammonites, and who sacrificed his daughter in fulfillment of a vow (Judges 11–12)

Jericho: a city in the Jordan Valley, seven miles north of the Dead Sea (see esp. Joshua 2; 6)

Jerub-Baal: another name for Gideon (see Judges 9)

Joash: the father of Gideon (Judges 6–8)

Jotham: the youngest of Gideon's seventy sons (Judges 9)

Kedesh: one of the cities of refuge (see Joshua 20:7; Judges 4:9-10)

Kenites: nomadic people who were known for their skill in metal working (Judges 1:16; 4:11, 17; 5:24)

Kenizzites: a tribe from the territory of Edom (Joshua 14:6, 14)

Kiriath Arba: also called Hebron, a city in the hill country that served as a city of refuge (Joshua 14:15; 15:13, 54; 20:7; 21:11: Judges 1:10)

Kiriath Sepher: another name for the city of Debir (Joshua 15:15-16; Judges 1:11-12)

Laish: A Canaanite city later known as Dan (Judges 18, esp. vv. 27-29)

Levirate marriage: a marriage between a widow and her dead husband's brother (see Deuteronomy 25:5-10; Ruth 1:11-13; 2:20; 3:9–4:12)

Machir: the oldest son of Ephraim, probably a leader in the conquest of Canaan (Joshua 13:31; 17:1, 3; Judges 5:14)

Makkedah: a city located about fifty miles southwest of Gilgal (see esp. Joshua 10:9-10, 16-28)

Manna: food provided by God for the people, beginning after the crossing of the Red Sea and ceasing after the crossing of the Jordan (Joshua 5:12)

Manoah: a Danite, the father of Samson (see esp. Judges 13)

Moab: a territory east of the Dead Sea (see Ruth 1)

Micah: an Ephraimite who erected a shrine in his house (Judges 17–18)

Mount Ebal: a mountain near Shechem from which curses were pronounced (Joshua 8:30-35)

Mount Gerizim: a mountain near Shechem from which blessings were pronounced (Joshua 8:30-35)

Mount Seir: a mountain southwest of the Dead Sea, in the territory of Edom (Joshua 11:17; 12:7; 15:10; 24:4; Judges 5:4)

Mount Tabor: a mountain on the boundary line between the tribes of Zebulun and Naphtali (Joshua 19:22; Judges 4; 8:18)

Naomi: the mother-in-law of Ruth (see Ruth)

Nazirites: persons dedicated to God who abstained from alcohol and did not cut their hair (see Judges 13)

Negev: the desert to the south of Canaan (see esp. Judges 1)

Ophrah: the home of Gideon (Joshua 18:23; Judges 6:11, 24; 8:27, 32; 9:5)

Othniel: the first judge in Israel (Joshua 15:17; Judges 1:13; 3:9-11)

Peniel: a city on the Jabbok River whose inhabitants were killed after refusing to aid Gideon (Judges 8:8-9, 17)

GLOSSARY OF TERMS

Peor: a mountain in Moab where Balak took Balaam to curse Israel (Joshua 22:17)

Philistines: a people who settled on the coast of Palestine and who were defeated by Samson (see esp. Judges 14–16)

Phinehas: the grandson of Aaron who had an important role in the conquest of Canaan (see esp. Joshua 22)

Promised Land: the territory bounded by the Mediterranean Sea on the west, the desert on the east and south, and the Lebanon mountains to the north

Rahab: a prostitute living in Jericho who hid the Israelite spies in her house (Joshua 2; 6:17, 23, 25)

Samson: a hero of the tribe of Dan who became a judge in Israel (Judges 13–16)

Shamgar: a Canaanite who became a deliverer of Israel (Judges 3:31; 5:6)

Shechem: the city where the covenant-renewal ceremony took place (see esp. Joshua 24)

Shekel: a piece of silver weighing about four ounces (Joshua 7:21)

Shiloh: a city in the hill country south of Shechem (see esp. Judges 21)

Shittim: a stopping-place for the Israelites before they entered Canaan, seven miles east of the Jordan River (Joshua 2:1; 3:1)

Sisera: the leader of a group of Canaanite kings; he was defeated by the troops of Deborah and Barak (Judges 4–5)

Succoth: a city near the Jordan River whose inhabitants refused aid to Gideon (Joshua 13:27; Judges 8)

Taanach: a Canaanite city in the hill country that was defeated by Joshua (Joshua 12:21; 17:11; 21:25; Judges 1:27; 5:19)

Timnah: a Philistine city during the days of Samson (see esp. Judges 14:2-7)

Timnath Serah: the home of Joshua, in the hill country of Ephraim (Joshua 19:50; 24:30)

Urim and Thummim: sacred lots (stones) that were used to discover the will of God (see Exodus 28:30; Joshua 7:14-18)

Valley of Achor: a riverbed located about five miles south of Jericho (Joshua 7:24-26; 15:7)

Waters of Merom: a brook northwest of the Sea of Galilee (Joshua 11:5, 7)

Zelophehad: a man from the tribe of Manasseh, whose daughters gained inheritance rights (Joshua 17:3)

About the Writer

The writer of these lessons is the Reverend Ray Newell, who served as the pastor of Westland United Methodist Church in Lebanon, Tennessee. For several years, Rev. Newell taught Bible and religion at Mount Union College, Alliance, Ohio.

CPSIA information can be obtained
at www.ICGtesting.com
Printed in the USA
BVHW052109021120
592172BV00008B/105